www.wadsworth.com

wadsworth.com is the World Wide Web site for Wadsworth and is your direct source to dozens of online resources.

At *wadsworth.com* you can find out about supplements, demonstration software, and student resources. You can also send email to many of our authors and preview new publications and exciting new technologies.

wadsworth.com
Changing the way the world learns®

The Wadsworth College Success Series

Campbell, *The Power to Learn: Helping Yourself to College Success,* 2nd Ed. (1997). ISBN: 0-534-26352-6

Clason and Beck, *On the Edge of Success* (2003). ISBN: 0-534-56973-0

Corey, *Living and Learning* (1997). ISBN: 0-534-50500-7

Gordon and Minnick, *Foundations: A Reader for New College Students,* 2nd Ed. (2002). ISBN: 0-534-52431-1

Holkeboer and Walker, *Right from the Start: Taking Charge of Your College Success,* 4th Ed. (2003). ISBN: 0-534-59967-2

Petrie and Denson, *A Student Athlete's Guide to College Success: Peak Performance in Class and in Life,* 2nd Ed. (2003). ISBN: 0-534-57000-3

Santrock and Halonen, *Your Guide to College Success: Strategies for Achieving Your Goals, Media Edition,* 2nd Ed. (2002). ISBN: 0-534-57205-7

Van Blerkom, *Orientation to College Learning,* 3rd Ed. (2002). ISBN: 0-534-57269-3

Wahlstrom and Williams, *Learning Success: Being Your Best at College & Life,* Media Edition, 3rd Ed. (2002). ISBN: 0-534-57314-2

The Freshman Year Experience™ Series

Gardner and Jewler, *Your College Experience: Strategies for Success,* Media Edition, 5th Ed. (2003). ISBN: 0-534-59382-8

Concise Media Edition, 4th Ed. (2001). ISBN: 0-534-55053-3
The Reader, 5th Ed. (2003). ISBN: 0-534-59985-0
Expanded Workbook Edition (1997). ISBN: 0-534-51897-4

Study Skills/Critical Thinking

Kurland, *I Know What It Says...What Does It Mean? Critical Skills for Critical Reading* (1995). ISBN: 0-534-24486-6

Longman and Atkinson, *CLASS: College Learning and Study Skills,* 6th Ed. (2002). ISBN: 0-534-56962-5

Longman and Atkinson, *SMART: Study Methods and Reading Techniques,* 2nd Ed. (1999). ISBN: 0-534-54981-0

Smith, Knudsvig, and Walter, *Critical Thinking: Building the Basics,* 2nd Ed. (2003). ISBN: 0-534-59976-1

Sotiriou, *Integrating College Study Skills: Reasoning in Reading, Listening, and Writing,* 6th Ed. (2002). ISBN: 0-534-57297-9

Van Blerkom, *College Study Skills: Becoming a Strategic Learner,* 4th Ed. (2003). ISBN: 0-534-57467-X

Watson, *Learning Skills for College and Life* (2001). ISBN: 0-534-56161-6

Student Assessment Tool

Hallberg, *College Success Factors Index,* http://success.wadsworth.com

On the Edge of Success

On the Edge of Success

Marmy A. Clason

Concordia University Wisconsin

John A. Beck

Concordia University Wisconsin

Australia • Canada • Mexico • Singapore • Spain • United Kingdom • United States

THOMSON
WADSWORTH

THOMSON
WADSWORTH

Executive Manager, College Success: *Annie Mitchell*
Assistant Editor: *Kirsten Markson*
Technology Project Manager: *Barry Connolly*
Advertising Project Manager: *Linda Yip*
Project Manager, Editorial Production: *Erica Silverstein*
Print/Media Buyer: *Rebecca Cross*
Permissions Editor: *Stephanie Keough-Hedges*
Production Service: *Anne Draus, Scratchgravel Publishing Services*

Printed in the United States of America
1 2 3 4 5 6 7 06 05 04 03 02

For more information about our products, contact us at:
Thomson Learning Academic Resource Center
1-800-423-0563

For permission to use material from this text, contact us by:
Phone: 1-800-730-2214 **Fax:** 1-800-730-2215
Web: http://www.thomsonrights.com

Library of Congress Control Number: 2002105206

ISBN 0-534-56973-0

Text and Cover Designer: *Lisa Mirski Devenish*
Photo Researcher: *Laura Molmud*
Copy Editor: *Frank Herbert*
Illustrator: *Gregory Draus*
Cover Image: *Image © 2002 Getty Images, Inc.*
Text and Cover Printer: *Banta*
Compositor: *Scratchgravel Publishing Services*

Wadsworth/Thomson Learning
10 Davis Drive
Belmont, CA 94002-3098
USA

Asia
Thomson Learning
60 Albert Street, #15-01
Albert Complex
Singapore 189969

Australia
Nelson Thomson Learning
102 Dodds Street
South Melbourne, Victoria 3205
Australia

Canada
Nelson Thomson Learning
1120 Birchmount Road
Toronto, Ontario M1K 5G4
Canada

Europe/Middle East/Africa
Thomson Learning
Berkshire House
168-173 High Holborn
London WC1V 7AA
United Kingdom

Latin America
Thomson Learning
Seneca, 53
Colonia Polanco
11560 Mexico D.F.
Mexico

Spain
Paraninfo Thomson Learning
Calle/Magallanes, 25
28015 Madrid, Spain

To my mother, Lorraine Beck, who taught me to be compassionate by modeling compassion.

To the whole Clason clan, who taught me the healing benefits of laughter.

Contents

Foreword

I provide this Foreword from two perspectives. The first is as a former probationary new college student (approximately 40 years ago). The second is from my present vantage point as a professor who has dedicated his whole career to leading a national movement to increase the time, energy, efforts, and resources directed by colleges and universities to helping new college students such as you. The future of our country depends on more of you having a successful first year that forms the basis of your college experience. That success makes you more likely to graduate, achieve your objectives, and be even more productive citizen leaders, family members, and employees in our society. I support this book's effort to achieve that broad-based set of social outcomes. This Foreword is written especially to provide testimony from me as to why I believe the authors of this book are "right on" in terms of both the objectives and the specific recommendations they present for helping probationary students.

First of all, I want you to know that I too was once a student on probation during my second semester in college in the spring of 1962. My only term on academic probation was a memorable experience. However, unlike your college or university, my college had no special intervention process or program for probationary students. We basically received a written edict from the dean of the college telling us we were on "academic pro," and if we did not get off in a semester, we would be booted out of the place. Believe me, I would never be writing this Foreword if I did not get off academic probation.

How did I get off without having a book such as this? Well, in brief, an outstanding, successful older student reached out to me and taught me how to be a successful college student. Luckily, with the help of this wiser student, I chose some professors for that term on academic probation who really engaged me. They opened up a whole new world of ideas, questions, challenges, and intellectual growth experiences that enhanced my self-esteem. I also received help from an outstanding faculty member who became my academic advisor after I had the good sense to leave my first advisor and choose one who had a keen interest in my welfare. In addition, the passage of time itself was a big help in allowing me to recover from homesickness and adjust to my new environment. You and I may have some experiences in common.

The authors of this book, Marmy Clason and Jack Beck, are two university faculty who are truly dedicated to helping probationary students be successful in college. Some of their colleagues might be more likely to write off such students, if not as lost causes, at least as more doubtful candidates for college success. I respect these two authors for their belief in the potential of students on probation. They recognize, as do I, that students grow at different rates and in different ways. Many students do not "get it" the first time around and end up on academic probation. One of the most striking characteristics of our American higher education system, compared with systems of other countries, is that ours is very forgiving. We give students additional chances to learn. I urge you to take advantage of this cultural and institutional advantage. It is an opportunity for a kind of academic redemption. Later in life, circumstances in employment and relationships may not be quite so forgiving and supportive.

Marmy Clason and Jack Beck are basing this book on the core concept of "the edge of success." This means the authors believe, as do I, that you already have the potential to be successful in college, or you would not have been admitted. You are just on the edge of using that potential. The key question here is: How do we get you to use your potential? I believe, and so do the authors, that using one's potential is a skill that can be taught. That is what this book is all about. I hope you consider their advice seriously. It has the power to help you fulfill your potential and transform the direction of your adult life. My bet is on Marmy Clason and Jack Beck because of their confidence in you and your potential. I am what you will be: living proof that probationary students can turn out just fine! Please allow yourself the opportunity to consider and practice the fine counsel they provide in this unique work. All the best to you in your college experience.

John N. Gardner
Executive Director, Policy Center on the First Year of College
Distinguished Professor of Educational Leadership
Brevard College

Senior Fellow,
National Resource Center on the First-Year Experience
and Students in Transition
Distinguished Professor Emeritus of Library and Information Science
University of South Carolina

Preface

On the Edge of Success is more than just the title of this textbook. It is our belief about students who are on academic probation. We do not view these individuals as students who have failed but as students who are about to succeed. Many of them will succeed when we affirm their self-worth, provide them with encouragement, and give them the tools to facilitate their success.

This positive perspective would not have been associated with probationary students prior to the mid-1980s. In the past, a student who earned a low grade point average for more than one semester was considered ripe for dismissal. The probationary warning was a mere formality signaling the student that it was time to pack for home. Today, more colleges and universities realize that many of these students are not destined to fail. They are students who can succeed if they address the poor study habits, poor health habits, and harmful relationship patterns that have interfered with their success.

This new perspective has led many universities to develop a course targeted specifically to the needs of students on probation. But what has been lacking is a textbook that directly addresses the needs of these students. Textbooks written for study skills courses and for first-year seminar courses don't adequately fit the needs of this unique population. That is why you have come to hold this textbook in your hand. Classes that address the needs of probationary students are often one-credit courses. Thus, this book is brief and fundamental in its presentation.

Schools may differ in their definition of academic underperformance, but the needs of the probationary student remain consistent across institutions of higher education regardless of their size or constituency. The students who are on academic probation often struggle with low self-esteem. We believe this problem must be tackled immediately to animate their desire for success. Thus, this book seeks to address these students with an affirming and encouraging tone throughout.

Students on probation must also accept responsibility for making changes in their lives. Therefore, this book regularly asks students to assess their past performance to determine where those changes need to occur.

Finally, the needs of students on academic probation are urgent. They need to make immediate changes in their habits to bolster their academic performance. Consequently, this book seeks to be practical by asking students to apply the tools in the text to their current coursework.

Look for the following features throughout the book:

- *Tone.* Each chapter challenges students to accept responsibility for previous shortcomings, while at the same time offering encouragement and support.
- *Topics.* This book covers the topics most important to rebuilding fundamental academic skills and attitudes.
- *Exercises.* Each chapter invites students to practice the skills and apply them through a series of critical and creative thinking exercises.
- *Journal.* Students have a chance to reflect on their changing attitudes and behaviors through guided journal suggestions.
- *On the Net.* Students may pursue additional ideas for success on the World Wide Web with the Internet sites recommended at the end of each chapter.

On the Edge of Success is more than just the title of this book. It is our belief about every student who reads this book.

Acknowledgments

It is with deep gratitude that we acknowledge those who have made a significant contribution to the development and production of this book. We are indebted to David Eggebrecht, Vice President of Academics at Concordia University Wisconsin, for his untiring support of first-year student programming on our campus. We also wish to acknowledge Elana Dolberg and Annie Mitchell, our editors, who had a vision for reaching these unique students at schools across the nation. We have deeply valued their insightful advice, thoughtful direction, and untiring encouragement. We also wish to thank the entire team at Wadsworth whose names appear on only one page of this book but whose influence is felt on every page. In that same light, we wish to thank Anne and Gregory Draus at Scratchgravel Publishing Services for overseeing the appearance and organization of this book. We also are indebted to John Gardner both for the foreword and for his continuing work on behalf of first-year students. He truly has provided the garden in which this idea might grow. Finally, we would like to thank the students we have met in our probation classes. Their candor, honesty, and suggestions have had an impact on every page. They have truly showed us what it means to be on the edge of success.

On the Edge of Success

1

See Yourself on the Edge of Success

You did it! You made a great decision when you decided to come to college. And no matter how you may be feeling at the moment, it is still the right place for you to be. You are in the process of earning a college degree. That degree will help you become the person you wish to be and allow you to realize the dreams you have dared to dream.

A college degree will make you a better thinker and a more independent learner. You will possess a higher degree of self-esteem and self-confidence. That refined thinking and confidence will have an impact on your employment and personal life. You will have a less erratic job history, earn more promotions, and report greater satisfaction with your work. You will have a higher income, save more money, and make better investments. Perhaps you didn't realize all these benefits of a college degree when you filled out your application, but these realities will become your own when the diploma is placed in your hand.

Let's be honest with each other. Graduating from college is important to you. You would not be reading this book if that were not so. Even though you are facing challenges, you are not giving up. You are fighting for your dream. The authors of this book have a deep respect for your tenacity and your passion. It is clear to us that you have not fallen over the edge. You are standing on the edge of success.

Am I really on the edge of success?

What can I do to be more successful?

EXERCISE

Recapture Your Dream

Let's begin by recapturing the dreams you have for your life following graduation. Take a blank sheet of paper and draw a line from one side to the other. On the left side of that line, put the year of your graduation. Let the right side of your time line be 10 years later. Between the two ends of the line, place the dreams you wish to realize in the 10 years following graduation. Do you want to purchase a new car or home? Do you want to start a family? When do you plan to start your new job? Do you plan to travel? How do you wish to change the world? What do you want your life to look like following graduation? See the example that follows. ●

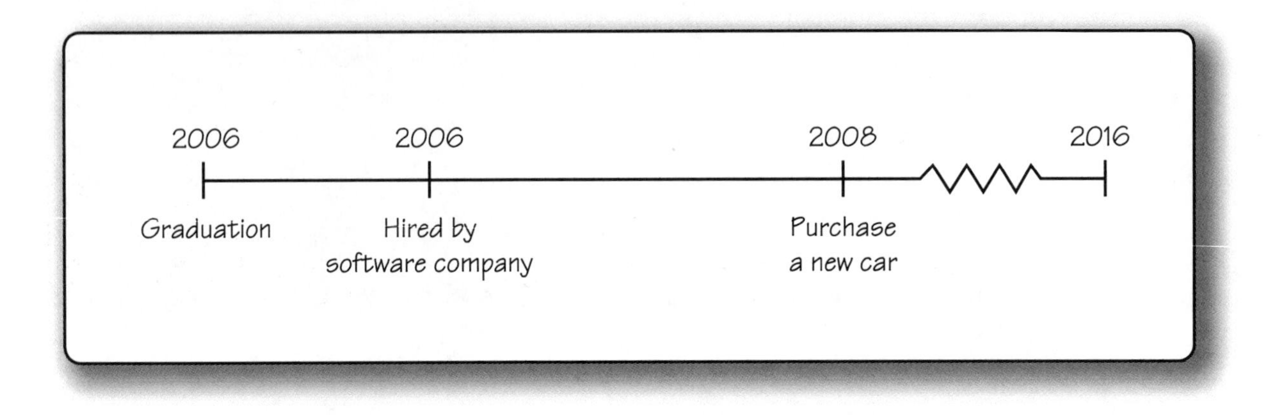

The fact that you have experienced some difficulty in your classwork does not mean that you will be unable to graduate from college. Many successful people have struggled in life and still achieved or exceeded their dreams. Here are some examples:

Louisa May Alcott, the famous author of *Little Women,* was told by an editor that her writings would never appeal to the public.

Famous composer Ludwig van Beethoven had a music teacher who said that as a composer, he was "hopeless."

Renowned scientist Sir Isaac Newton did work in elementary school that was labeled "poor."

The inventor who brought us electricity, Thomas Edison, was told by his teacher that he was too stupid to learn.

We would not have pasteurized milk without Louis Pasteur. But he was given a rating of "mediocre" in chemistry at Royal College.

PhotoDisc/gettyimages, 2002

Walt Disney was fired by a newspaper editor because he had "no good ideas."

Michael Jordan did not make his high school basketball team in his sophomore year; his coach said he wasn't good enough.

Emily Dickinson wrote 1800 poems, but only 7 were published in her lifetime.

Charles Schultz, creator of Charlie Brown, failed algebra, Latin, English, and physics in high school. His cartoons were rejected by the yearbook staff of his high school.

All of these notable members of our society were told that they were failures, but in reality, they were on the edge of success.[1]

You are on the edge of success. Do your teachers doubt that? Does your school doubt that? Do you doubt that? Still, it is true. You are on

1. Adapted from Larson, M. E. (1973). Humbling cases for career counselors. *Phi Delta Kappan, LIV,* 374.

the edge of success. You may not think so at the moment. After all, the school has questioned your ability to succeed. Perhaps that makes you feel angry or discouraged. But does that mean are you are destined to fail? No. Students may earn low grades for many reasons. Health or relationship problems may have complicated your time in school. Perhaps you have struggled with the use of your time. But low grades do not mean you are a failure.

This book will help you find what stands between you and your success. It will give you direction and encouragement. We challenge you to read this book, do the exercises, and apply the techniques in your classes. Remember, your past grades do not determine your future success. You do. Success is within your grasp.

Success is no accident. It is too important to be left to chance. That is why this book is about designing your success. Let's begin by looking at a tool we call the "pyramid of success." The pyramid makes it clear that personal success is a product of many components that

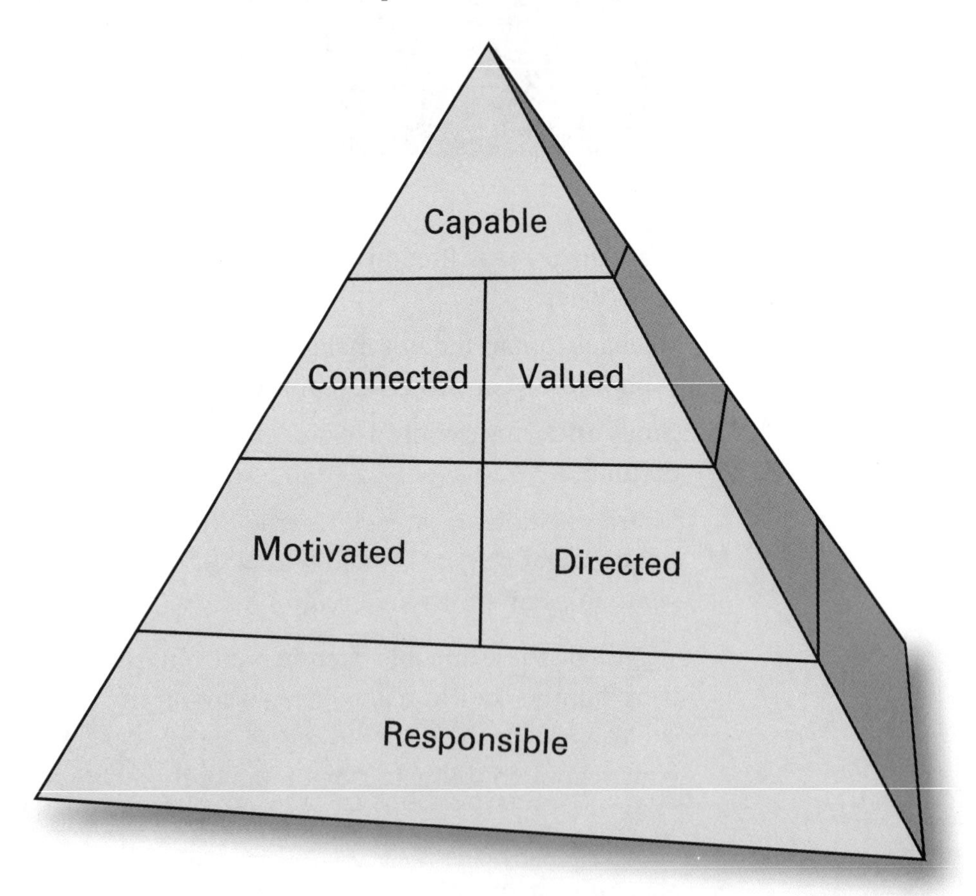

complement and build on one another. If any block within the pyramid is weak or missing, the structure of the pyramid is less stable. Then both your sense of well-being and your potential for success will suffer.

Let's look at the pyramid and see how you can apply it to yourself. Picture yourself standing on top of it. How stable do the blocks feel beneath your feet?

Responsible

The successful student is a responsible student. This is the foundation of the pyramid. It may be hard to think of yourself as being less than responsible, but you cannot move to the top of the pyramid without this foundation. Responsible students are able to own their past mistakes, make a commitment to change, and consistently use the tools and resources that are available to foster their success.

Motivated

The successful student is a motivated student. No one can get excited about your education for you. You need to make a personal and emotional investment in your future. You have to want it. When you do, you will be looking for ways to make it happen.

Directed

The successful student is directed. Sometimes you need a map when driving to a new destination. A map shows the way to your destination by guiding your journey. If you want to get to the top of the pyramid, you will need a map. That map will consist of clear and specific goals that direct you to your destination. If you are in the habit of setting goals and planning, you are on the right track. If you are not, this book will help you do it.

Connected

The successful student is connected to his or her community. You will not feel whole unless you are linked to others who value and support you on this journey. This community may be your family, friends, or a significant other. These people will support you on the way to the next step. Let's make sure you have a support group in place.

Valued

The successful student feels a strong sense of self-esteem. You may have allowed your circumstances to color the way you see yourself. For example, if you got a D on an exam, you may have seen yourself as a D person. This is not true. The D is a grade. It measures your understanding of a topic at a given moment. It says nothing about your value as a person. Appreciate yourself for the unique person you are because you are much more than a grade on a test.

Capable

Finally, the successful student is able to blend each component of the pyramid into a successful working whole. Each component of the pyramid is a step toward the top. If any steps are missing, the climb is difficult if not impossible. This book will help you stabilize your base, build your steps, and move to the top. You will find success when you combine what you have learned into a working whole.

How do the blocks look in your pyramid? Some are very strong. They need only minor editing. Of course, there are other blocks that need some work. Let's work together to identify your strengths and weaknesses so that you can climb the pyramid of success. Remember, your past grades do not determine your future success. You do.

CRITICAL REFLECTION EXERCISE

Your Life on the Edge of Success

In the pyramid that follows, write in the components for success as seen in the earlier illustration. Now, put a highlighter in your hand and visualize yourself climbing the pyramid from bottom to top. Pause at each level to reflect on your life at the moment. For example, ask yourself if you are a responsible person. If you believe that you are fully responsible, fill in the entire block. If you feel that you have some work to do in this area, fill in only that percentage of the block you think you have in place. Do this for each step of the pyramid to develop a picture of your starting point today. ●

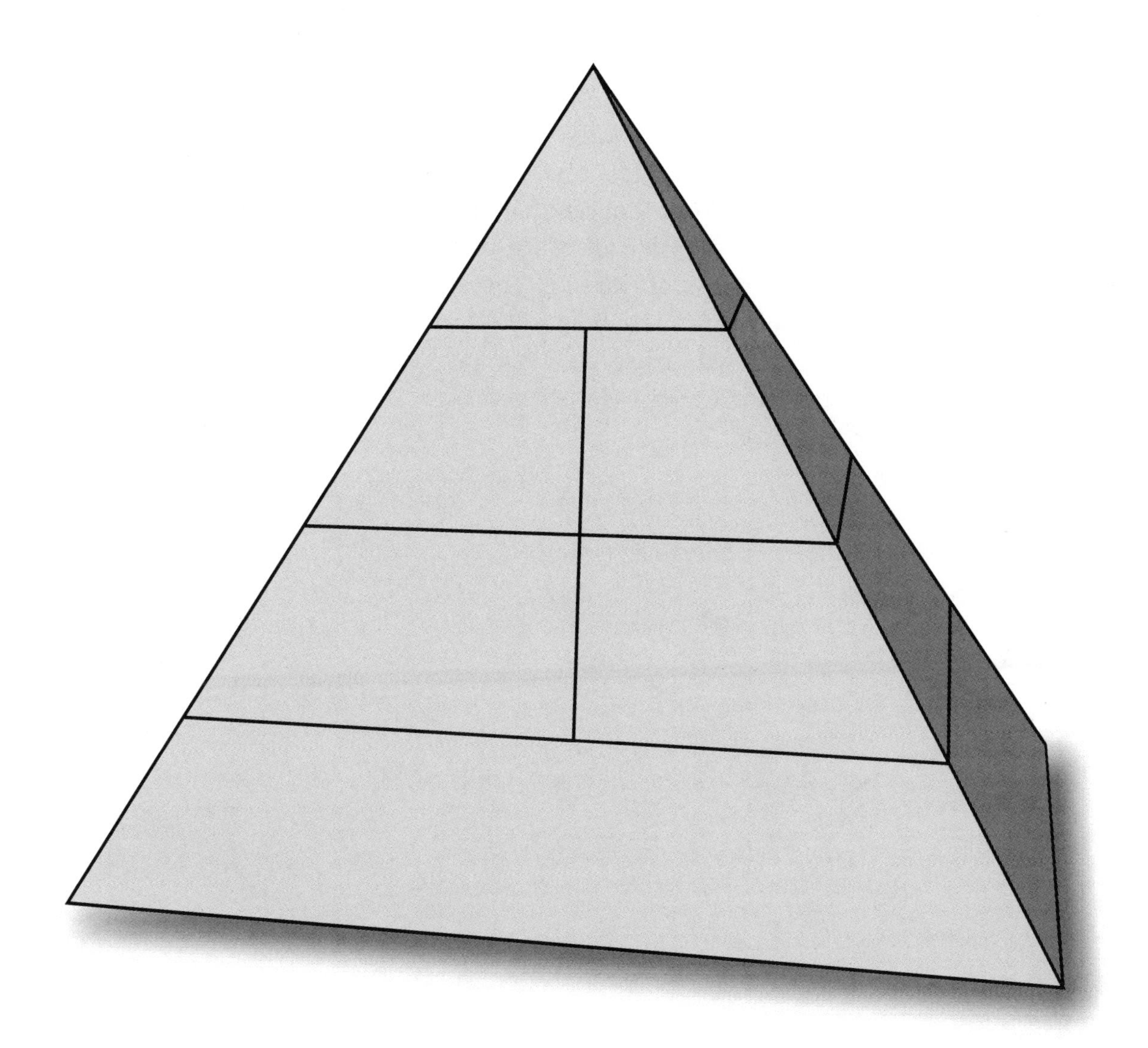

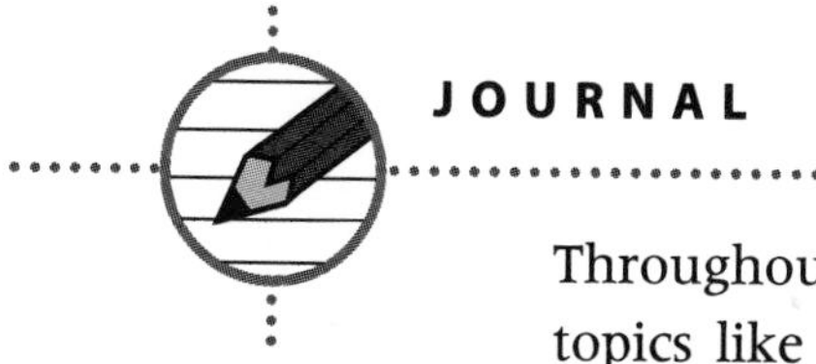

JOURNAL

Throughout this book, we will invite you to write brief reflections on topics like this. Be sure to save these journal entries. They will be a record of your growth and change.

Now it is time to put your picture into words. Look again at the way you have filled in the pyramid. Write about the things you are already doing to make yourself a more successful student. Begin with the words, "I am on the edge of success because . . ." Then go on to write about the portions of the pyramid you have filled in. ●

ON THE NET

Throughout this book, we will also invite you to consult the Internet on the topic of your success. Two sites will be of continuing help to you. The first is Your College Success Resource Center found at www.success.wadsworth.com. Click on "Discipline Resources" and explore the possibilities of this site. The second site we recommend is www.mindtools.com. Here you will also find a number of connections and links that will foster your success. You can also find additional resources and exercises for *On the Edge of Success* at http://info.wadsworth.com/clason. ●

2

Discover Your Habits

How did I get here?

What habits do I need to change?

What does your morning routine look like? Chances are you do the same things morning after morning. Your ritual may include taking a shower, brushing your teeth, eating breakfast, and going to class. This isn't the only way to begin your day. But it is your way. We are all creatures of habit.

Your desire to succeed means that you will have to change some old habits. Those are the habits that interfere with your climb up the pyramid of success. Habits can be hard to change. But remember that we are talking about habits, not the nature of who you are. You may have been born with brown eyes. That is part of who you are. It is not something you can change. We are talking about habits like missing classes, starting a paper the day before it is due, or even eating a candy bar for breakfast. You were not born with those habits. Those habits that interfere with your success need to be changed.

When your academic routine isn't working, it is important to examine what behaviors are interfering with your success. At the base of the pyramid of success is responsibility. Part of being a responsible student is reviewing the habits that make up a typical week for you in college. You may feel ready, even eager to move up the pyramid, but it is essential that we take time to examine your past habits. Unless you truly discover how your habits have contributed to your present state, you won't know what to fix. If your bicycle chain falls off, putting air in the tires does not fix the problem. Trying to fix something that is not broken and leaving broken what needs to be fixed only lead to frustration and disappointment. Let's discover your challenges.

CRITICAL REFLECTION PAPER

Discover Your Challenges

We saw in the previous chapter and its exercises that you have a lot going for you. That has not changed. Now let's discover your challenges. What follows is a checklist of habits that may have interfered with your chances for success in the past. Since you are the real expert in your life, we need your help. Carefully read the list and review your own habits. When a statement sounds like you, check it. Don't become worried or feel bad if you check many of the statements. In fact, being honest with yourself about your past behavior is a sign of maturity and responsibility. Stay with this inventory even if you feel a bit uncomfortable. Remember that admitting a problem is not a weakness! When you have completed the inventory, see the directions for completing a critical reflection paper.

Goal Setting and Motivation

- ❑ I am uncertain about my major.
- ❑ I don't feel motivated to do homework.
- ❑ I have trouble setting goals.
- ❑ I have trouble achieving the goals I have set.
- ❑ I don't know what motivates me.
- ❑ I don't have a written plan for success.

Time Management

- ❑ My class attendance needs improvement.
- ❑ I frequently sleep during the day.
- ❑ I have difficulty organizing my work.
- ❑ I have trouble with procrastination.
- ❑ I am easily distracted from my work.
- ❑ I find that sports, parties, or extracurricular activities interfere with my schoolwork.

- ❑ I spend too much time watching TV, playing video games, or surfing the Net.
- ❑ I don't make daily lists of things "to do."
- ❑ I don't make a weekly schedule for work, studying, classes, and free time.

Campus Resources

- ❑ I am nervous about visiting my teachers in their offices.
- ❑ I am unaware of all the support services offered on my campus.
- ❑ I am not sure from which kind of teacher I learn best.

Learning Styles

- ❑ I know that everyone learns differently, but I don't know in which ways I learn best.
- ❑ I have a difficult time learning from certain teachers.
- ❑ I don't understand why some people learn more easily than I do.
- ❑ I don't know how to study using my learning strengths.

Reading Strategies

- ❑ I frequently must reread portions of an assignment to understand it.
- ❑ I read too slowly.
- ❑ I don't have a system for remembering what I read.
- ❑ I am easily distracted when I read.
- ❑ I read in the same place that I relax.
- ❑ I don't begin reading the chapter of a book by scanning headings, graphs, and illustrations.
- ❑ I do most of my reading at night.

Note Taking

- ❑ I have trouble paying attention during class.
- ❑ I have only one method of taking notes for all my classes.
- ❑ I don't complete the assigned readings for my classes.

PhotoDisc/gettyimages, 2002

- ❑ Days pass before I review the notes I have taken.
- ❑ I review my notes by reading them over and over again.

Exams

- ❑ I usually start studying for an exam the day before it's given.
- ❑ I don't participate in a study group.
- ❑ I prepare for all my exams by just rereading my notes.
- ❑ I run out of time when taking an exam.
- ❑ My anxiety causes me to forget information that I have studied.
- ❑ I begin all my exams by answering the first question.
- ❑ I stay up very late, sometimes all night, to study for an exam.
- ❑ I have trouble remembering things for an exam.

Writing Papers

- ❑ I am not sure what resources to use when I research a topic in the library.
- ❑ I don't begin writing a paper by writing an outline.
- ❑ I don't reread and edit a paper before I give it to the teacher.
- ❑ My papers receive lower grades because of spelling mistakes or errors in grammar.
- ❑ My papers receive lower grades because they do not flow logically from paragraph to paragraph.
- ❑ I have difficulty picking a topic for some of my papers.
- ❑ I tend to write my papers one or two days before they are due.

Health

- ❑ I have a habit of sleeping during the day and staying up very late at night.
- ❑ I am under a lot of stress and I am not sure what to do with it.
- ❑ I don't have free time planned during my day.
- ❑ I skip breakfast a lot.
- ❑ I don't eat well-balanced meals.
- ❑ I frequently use a stimulant like caffeine to stay awake during the day.
- ❑ Traumatic events from my past are interfering with my ability to succeed today.

Relationships

- ❑ I am homesick.
- ❑ My relationship with my roommates is affecting my grades.
- ❑ I don't have any friends.
- ❑ My friends often get me into trouble.
- ❑ I am afraid to interact with my instructors.
- ❑ My boyfriend/girlfriend depends on me too much.
- ❑ I depend on my boyfriend/girlfriend too much.
- ❑ My family does not support my success.
- ❑ I worry about the health of my relationships.

Let's Write

Now that you have had the opportunity to reflect on some of the challenges blocking your climb up the pyramid of success, let's write your story. Prepare a two- to three-page reflection paper in which you identify and describe the most significant challenges you face. This paper will be more than a list. Tell the particulars of your story. For example, don't just mention that you have difficulty with procrastination. Tell us how that looks in your life. Don't be afraid to explain its consequences and your feelings about it. ●

CRITICAL THINKING EXERCISE

Picture Your Life

The habits you have checked in the "Discovering Your Challenges" exercise don't operate in isolation from one another. One poor habit may lead to another. For example, if you stayed up late on Thursday night, you may find it very hard to get to your early-morning chemistry class. If you do make it, you may find it hard to pay attention in class and take notes. And that may mean a lower test grade 2 weeks later. Here is how that looks in a diagram.

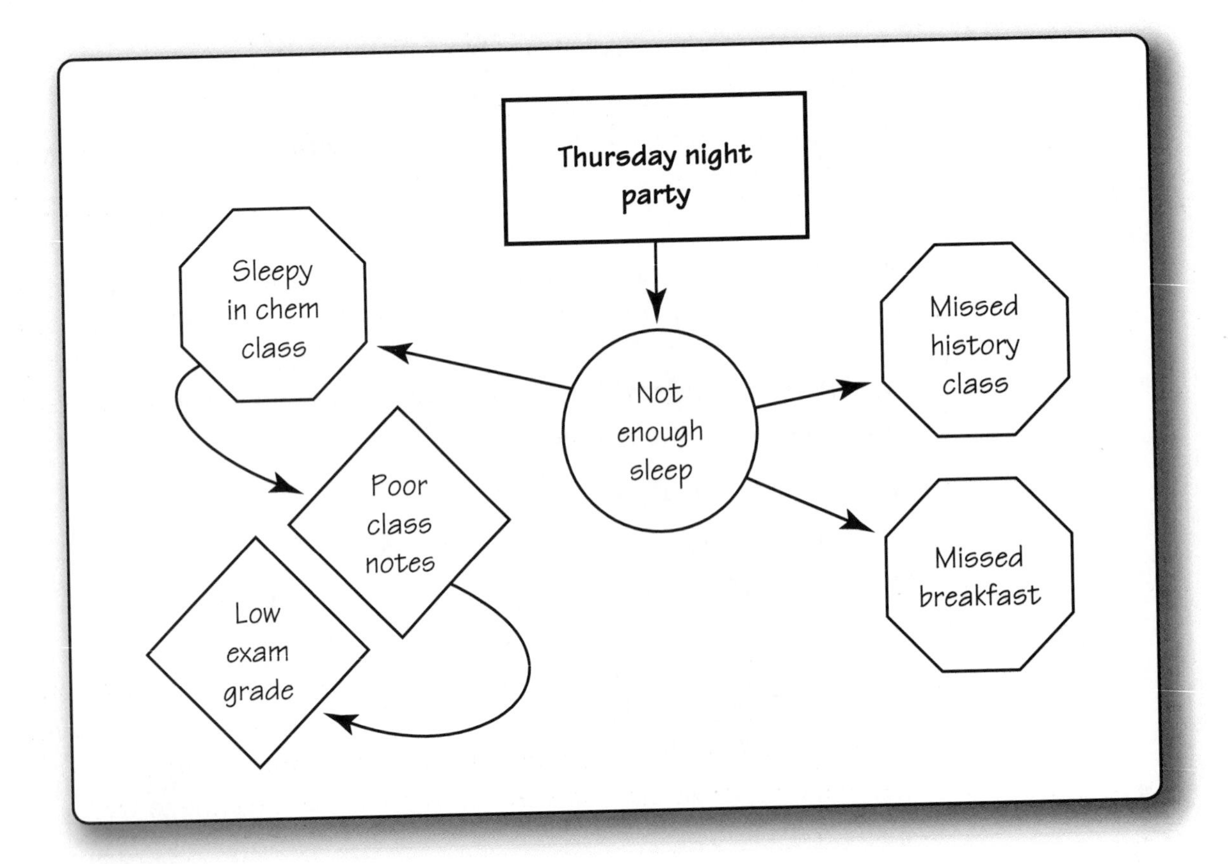

Box 2.1

Computing Your GPA

Your grade point average (GPA) is a mathematical average of your course grades. This is one of the ways your school records your performance. It is easy to compute your current GPA by using the following procedure. For each course, multiply the number of credit hours by the number assigned to that grade value. Check with your registrar's office for the numbers assigned to grade values on your campus. In a basic four-point system, the values are as follows: A = 4, B = 3, C = 2, D = 1, and F = 0. For example, if you received an A in a three-credit history course, you would multiply $3 \times 4 = 12$. The number 12 in this case represents the "quality points" you have earned for this class. Do this for each of your classes. Then add up the quality points and divide them by the total number of credit hours you took that semester. This is your GPA. See the following example.

Course	Grade	Credit Hours	Grade Value	Quality Points
History	B	3	3	9
Chem.	C	4	2	8
English	D	3	1	3
Math	B	3	3	9
Total		13		29

$29 \div 13 = 2.23$ GPA

Let's draw a picture from your life. Place one of the habits you wish to change inside a box. Then, using arrows and shapes, illustrate how that one habit may link to others you wish to change. The goal of this exercise is to illustrate visually how some of the habits you checked earlier influence one another. ●

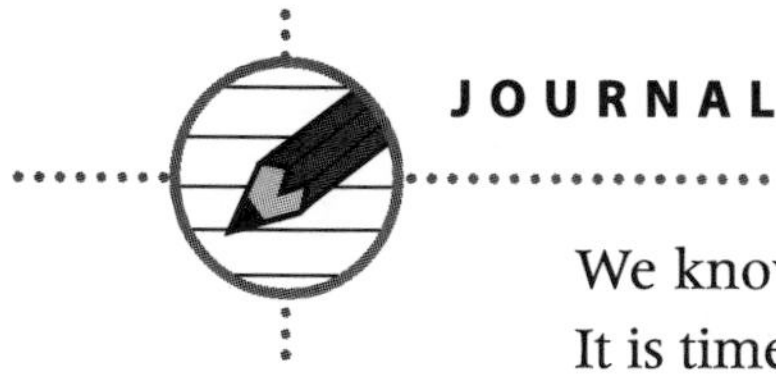

JOURNAL

We know that you have made attempts to improve your habits before. It is time to reflect in your journal again. What have you tried to change in the past? How have you attempted to make those changes? What has worked? What has not worked? What are you willing to try? ●

ON THE NET

Go to Your College Success Resource Center at www.success.wadsworth.com. Click on "Discipline Resources," then look under "Resource Web Links." Here, you will find a variety of links that address issues you checked earlier. Bookmark sites or record the addresses of sites that you plan to review in the future. You can also find additional resources and exercises for *On the Edge of Success* at http://info.wadsworth.com/clason. ●

3

Begin to Change

John knew he needed to change. Things were not going well for John in chemistry and composition class. He failed his last chemistry test, and he did not complete the last assignment for his composition class. To make matters worse, he had not attended either class for the last 2 weeks. John looked down at the floor, sighed, and said, "I'm just not motivated. Where do I go from here?"

Have you said that to yourself? Have you wondered where you are going from here? That question invites conversation on three related topics: motivation, goal setting, and decision making. Look back to the pyramid of success. You will see that motivation and goal setting are found on the same level. You need both the energy to move and a direction to move if you are going to make a change in your life.

Where am I going?

How can I be more motivated?

How can I set achievable goals?

How can I make better decisions?

Motivation

Motivation is the inner drive that moves us to act. When you say that you are unmotivated, you are not describing the essence of who you are. You are describing your relationship to a specific task or goal. There are times in your life when you are highly motivated. For example, Jason may not be motivated to get up for his early-morning composition class, but he is very motivated to get up for an early-morning flight to a spring break destination!

The same is true for you in your life. Let's think about what does or does not motivate you to accomplish a specific task.

As human beings, we are motivated by a variety of wants, needs, and fears. Here is a short list of things that may move you to act on a goal.

- Sense of pride
- Need for money
- Desire for accomplishment
- Religious or moral conviction
- Desire for power
- Need for respect
- Fear of failure
- Fear of disappointing others
- Fear of personal pain
- Sense of loyalty
- Spirit of adventure

Consider what may motivate you to learn how to rock climb. Both authors of this text have learned the basics of rock climbing. What motivated us to pursue this training despite the cost and personal risk? The answer is found in the following mind map.

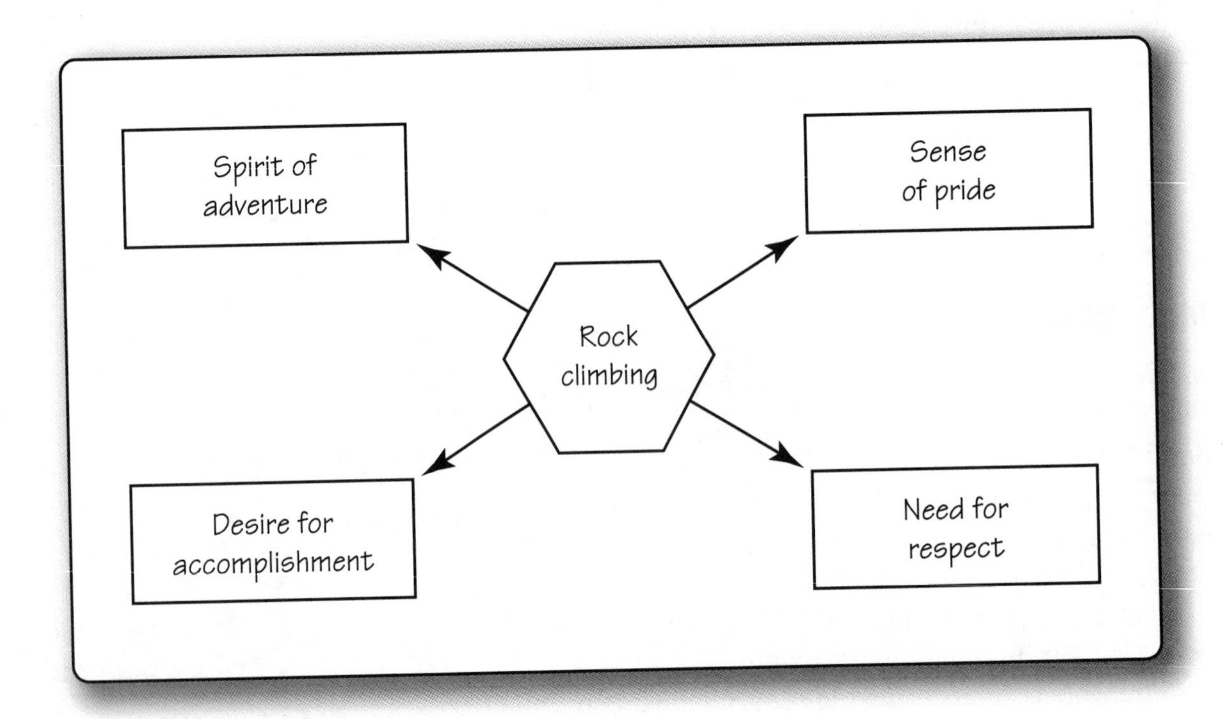

CRITICAL REFLECTION EXERCISE

Picture Your Motivation

Now it is your turn. In the empty symbol that follows, write something that you were highly motivated to do and have accomplished. This could be participation in athletics, the successful completion of a class, or volunteer work. From the preceding list and from your own experience, create a mind map that shows what motivated you to complete the task. ●

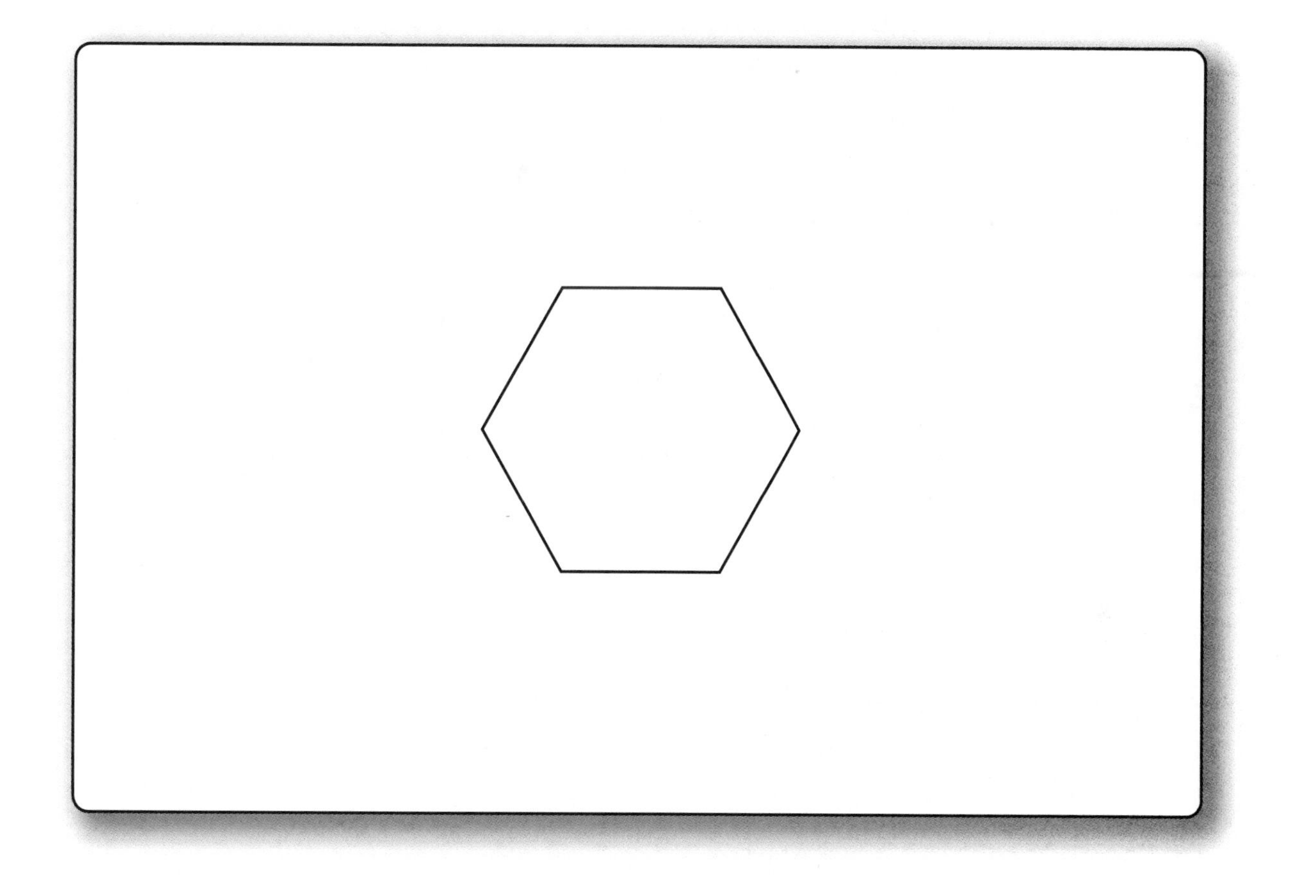

Goal Setting and Decision Making

Motivation is important, but motivation is not enough. You need to channel and focus the energy of your motivation so that you can accomplish what you desire. Undirected activity can accomplish as little as doing nothing. You may be highly motivated to make a cake, but the haphazard mixing of various ingredients is unlikely to give you the treat you want. You need a written recipe, a plan to accomplish the results you desire. In many respects, that is what goal setting is all

Box 3.1

Set Yourself Up for Success: Easy Daily Goals

One way to get started in this process that will help you feel some early satisfaction is to set up daily goals for yourself. All of us have some small things we can do every day that benefit us. What are some healthy things you can do for yourself every day? Write them down. Post them in a prominent place. Make them easy but helpful. You will be surprised at the satisfaction you feel from accomplishing these easy daily goals. Consider the following examples.

Exercise for 15 minutes each day.

Eat one serving of fruit and one serving of vegetables each day.

Watch only 2 hours of TV each day.

Say aloud two positive things that happened today.

about. It is a written recipe for success. This is why the words *motivated* and *directed* are on the same level in the pyramid of success. Goals direct you and channel the energy of your motivation.

There are several steps to the process of goal setting and decision making. We will introduce them to you and then invite you to participate in this very important process. Once you have a clearer picture of your goals, then you will be able to answer the question: Where am I going?

Step One: Get the Big Picture

The first step in setting a goal is getting the big picture of your life. It is easy to get caught up in the present crisis and respond to it without considering what you ultimately want out of life. So what do you want out of life? Think about it in terms of intention statements. I want to do better in my composition class. I want to help homeless families. I want to own my own house by the time I am 30 years old. I want to become a nurse. I want to buy a new car after I graduate from college. You may have similar plans for your life. Intention statements like these address many aspects of your life such as the following:

School

Career

Finances

Family

Relationships

Health

Recreation

Spiritual growth

Community service

Politics

Your intention statements describe where you want your life to go. All the best evidence suggests that you are more likely to get to that place if you formally state your intentions to get there.

Step Two: Write a Goal Statement

The second step employs the raw material generated during the first step. Now it is time to make your intention statement a goal statement. This step sharpens your thinking on your goal. It also improves your chances of achieving the plan. Well-written goals have five characteristics. You can remember them using the acronym SMART.

Specific Make your goal statement focused and clear. For example, "I want to do better in my composition class" is less specific than "I will achieve a higher grade in my composition class." Be sure to avoid using words like *try, think, hope,* or *should.*

Measured The best goal statements can be measured. This means they contain a value against which you can measure your progress. "I will achieve a grade of B or higher in my composition class."

Accepted Others may support your intentions, but they cannot be the sole reason for pursuing a goal. You must accept the goal as your own. Make sure that your goals spring from and are linked to your internal motivation and desires. "I will achieve a grade of B or higher in my composition class so that I can maintain my athletic scholarship."

Realistic Accomplishing a goal means changes in your life. But the changes cannot be so great that they threaten your relationships, your physical well-being, or your mental health. Your goal must be reachable. Reach high, but don't set yourself up for failure. Not every student will get an A in that composition class. If that grade goal is not realistic for you, set your goal so that it is practically within your reach. "I will achieve a grade of B or higher in my composition class."

Timed Finally, make sure your goal is set within a time frame. Set a limit for the goal. It may refer to the number of times you will do something or the date by which you intend to accomplish it. "I will achieve a grade of B or higher in my composition class by the close of this semester so that I can maintain my athletic scholarship."

Step Three: Develop an Action Plan

Now it is time to turn your goal statements into an action plan. An action plan identifies the specific tasks or steps you can take to accomplish your goal. The process that leads to your action plan involves three components: defining the challenges, brainstorming possible resources, and evaluating possible actions.

Various obstacles may stand in your way. The first component of this process asks you to define all the possible challenges that stand in the way of your goal. Next, brainstorm possible resources that could defeat the challenges you have named. Finally, it is time to evaluate the possible actions that would result in the successful achievement of your goal. Here is how that might look in connection with the following goal statement.

Goal: I will get a grade of B or higher in my composition class by the close of this semester so I can maintain my athletic scholarship.

Challenges	Brainstorming Resources	Evaluation of Possible Actions
I have trouble getting up for class.	Alarm clock Roommate	I will set my alarm clock for 7:15 A.M. Before I go to sleep, I will turn the volume up very high and put it across the room. Then I will have to get up to get rid of the noise. I will also ask my roommate to check up on me.
I don't understand the textbook.	Get a tutor. Ask someone who took the class last semester. Take a lower-level composition class.	I like the idea of one-on-one help from a tutor. I can work this into my time-management plan.

Step Four: Decide on an Action Plan

Once you have thought your way through the challenges and possible actions, you will be ready to decide on an action plan. This process puts the spotlight on the actions you need to take to accomplish your goal. Here is how your decisions might look at the completion of the process.

My Action Plan

Goal: I will get a grade of B or higher in my composition class by the close of this semester so I can maintain my athletic scholarship.

To achieve this goal, I will:

1. Get a weekly tutor.
2. Set up tutoring appointments in my time-management plan.
3. Set my alarm clock and leave it across the room so I know I will wake up in time for class.

Step Five: Implement the Action Plan

Writing out the goal statement and deciding on an action plan will position you for success. Now all you need to do is follow through on the plan. That means holding yourself accountable. This comes more easily for some than for others. Here are some things that you can do in this regard. Post the written goal in a highly visible location like your door or your bathroom mirror. Consider sharing your goal with a friend and ask for his or her support and encouragement in accomplishing it.

Being flexible also helps you achieve your goal. Goals are designed to be guides, not brutal taskmasters. You may need to adjust your action plan a bit as you implement it. That kind of thoughtful flexibility may actually help you accomplish your goal.

You also need to discover and maintain your motivation for this goal. Earlier in the chapter, we discussed a method for identifying your motivation for a task. Now would be a good time to draw a box and identify what motivates you to accomplish the goal before you.

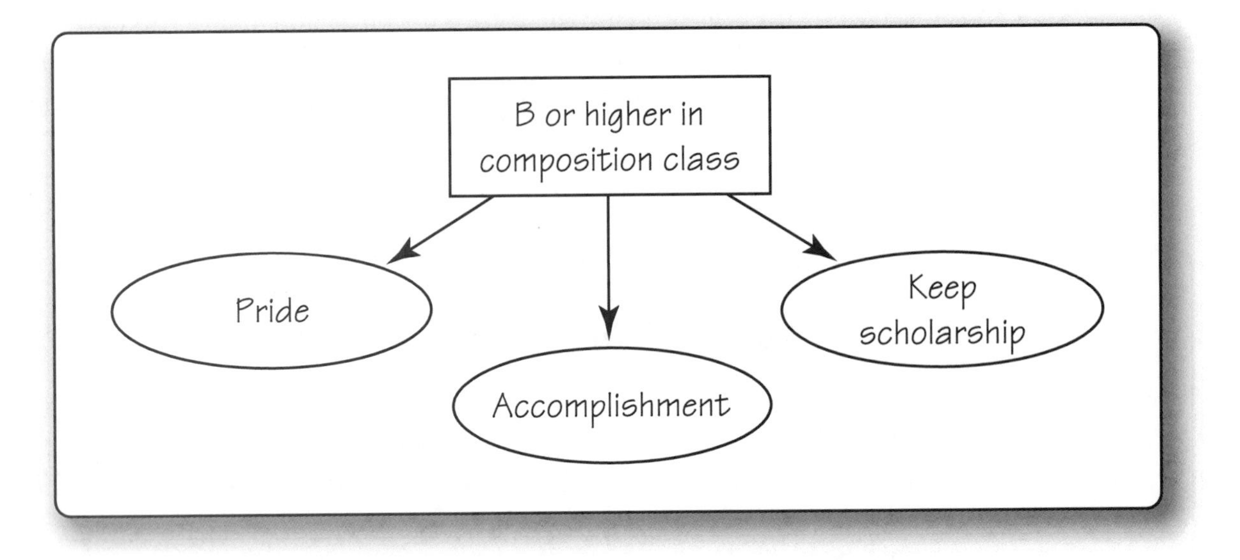

Finally, be ready to celebrate! Reward yourself for achievements made every step along the way. This will build your self-esteem and your momentum. Planning a reward is a great motivator. After you have completed a task that moves you toward your goal, be sure to celebrate.

PhotoDisc/gettyimages, 2002

Box 3.2

Still Feeling Unmotivated?

Are you still not feeling motivated? Are you having difficulty accomplishing your goals or daily tasks? Asking yourself the following three questions may help you discover the problem.

1. Can you focus? If you lack motivation or have trouble completing your tasks, it may be an external problem rather than an internal issue. If you cannot focus on a task, it is unlikely you will be able to complete it. For example, noise from TV or roommates or children may prevent you from attending to your task.
2. Are you able? You may feel a sense of motivation and have a clear goal in mind. But if you lack the ability to perform a key component of a task, you will be unable to complete it. For example, you may truly want to finish your research paper. But if you lack the ability to conduct an effective library search, you will be unable to complete the task.
3. Are you satisfied? You must feel satisfaction when your task, large or small, is completed. If you don't feel satisfaction, your motivation will be very low. For example, if you chose a major only because your parents wanted you to have that major, you are less likely to feel satisfaction in completing the coursework leading to that career.

You are on the edge of change. That change will occur when you are motivated to modify your life, are directed with goals, and have decided on an action plan. Remember, you need both the energy to move and a direction to move if you are going to make a change in your life.

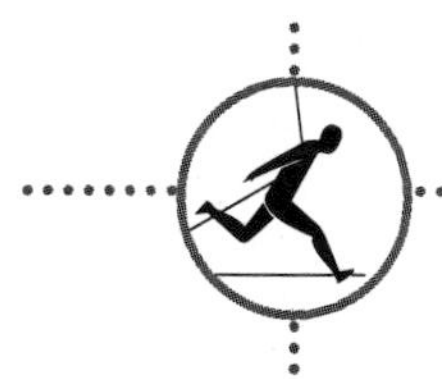

CRITICAL THINKING EXERCISE

Develop Your Action Plan

Now let's make this real in your life. Follow these steps. They will lead you to a well-written goal statement and action plan. Don't get discouraged. Just as with most things, practice will speed and improve the process.

Step One: Get the Big Picture

Now it is your turn to get the big picture in your life. You will need a pack of sticky notes or some small squares of paper. Write one intention statement on each slip of paper. Remember, give yourself the freedom to think and dream about your life. What do want to do? How do you want to live? What do you want to be? What do you want to accomplish? Place the statements on the desk in front of you and rearrange them by topic or time frame.

Step Two: Write a Goal Statement

Pick an intention statement that relates to your success this semester. Write out the first draft of the goal statement and check it against the SMART process. If your first draft has the quality listed, put a check in the box. Edit your first draft for any boxes not checked.

First Draft of Goal Statement:

____

____

____

- ❏ Specific
- ❏ Measured
- ❏ Accepted
- ❏ Realistic
- ❏ Timed

Edited Draft of Goal Statement:

____

____

____

Step Three: Develop an Action Plan

Using the goal from step two, develop and write an action plan that will lead to the completion of your goal.

Goal: ______________________________

Challenges	Brainstorming Resources	Evaluation of Possible Actions

Step Four: Decide on an Action Plan

My Action Plan

Goal: ____

____

To achieve this goal, I will:

____

____

____

____

____

____

____

EXERCISE

Implement Your Action Plan with a Contract

The action plan you have just written can be put in the form of a contract. By developing a contract with a professional on your campus who is concerned about your success, you will enhance your chances of following through on your intentions. Seek out your advisor, your instructor, or another professional on campus who is willing to help hold you accountable to your plan. Discuss your action plans with this person. Then compose a contract that restates the action plan that both you and your mentor will sign. ●

CRITICAL REFLECTION EXERCISE

Write a Personal Mission Statement

Another way of articulating your life goals is by a personal mission statement. If you have never seriously considered how you want your life to be, this is a good place to start. Stephen Covey describes a personal mission statement as a paragraph in which you describe the kind of person you would like to be and define the key things you wish to accomplish in life. If you would like to learn more about developing your own personal mission statement, see Stephen Covey's *The Seven Habits of Highly Successful People* (New York: Simon & Schuster, 1989). Remember that getting the big picture means thinking about yourself, how you want to live your life, and what kind of person you want to be. ●

JOURNAL

Change can be difficult. Pick a time in your life when you have made a successful change. Write about the circumstances of your change. Describe what motivated you and what procedure you used to bring about that change in your life. ●

ON THE NET

The Internet is another rich source of information on motivation and goal setting. Go to www.mindtools.com. Click on the menu bar that reads "How to Use Time Effectively," then click on the link to the exercises titled "Personal Goal Setting—Planning to Achieve." Read through the pages on how to set goals and think about your own goals and how you will achieve them. You can also find additional resources and exercises for *On the Edge of Success* at http://info.wadsworth.com/clason. ●

4

Manage Your Time Efficiently

You are about to read one of the most important chapters in this book. Successful college students have repeatedly said that time management was critical to their climb up the pyramid of success. Let's take the action plan you designed in the previous chapter and set it to work on each day of your week.

Some people mistakenly assume that they were "born" to be poor time managers. This is not the case. We all have 24 hours each day. We all make choices about how we use those 24 hours. That is why we are calling your use of time a *habit*. This chapter invites you to carefully inspect that habit. You may find that your habit is sound at many levels. You may also find dimensions of the habit that need to be changed.

Do you forget when assignments are due? Do you run out of time when working on a project? Are you easily distracted from your work? These are habits that you can change. When you were in high school, much of your day was planned for you. You may not have had much practice in planning the use of your time. This chapter will give you some practice and empower your success by giving you tools with which to evaluate, organize, and edit your time-use habits.

How do I use my time?

How can I become better organized?

How can I limit distractions?

How can I avoid procrastination?

Estimate Your Time Use

Let's get started with a look at the way you see yourself. Estimate the amount of time you spend in a typical week doing the following, and add them up. Don't worry about being too specific. Just give your general impressions.

Time in Class	______ hours
Studying	______ hours
Work	______ hours
Commuting	______ hours
Family Time	______ hours
Volunteer Work	______ hours
Exercise	______ hours
Athletics	______ hours
Social Time with Friends	______ hours
Sleeping	______ hours
Eating	______ hours
Grooming, Dressing, Cleaning	______ hours
Fun (TV, music, dating, computer, phone, hobbies, shopping)	______ hours
Other	______ hours
Total Hours	______ (Do not exceed 168 hours!!)

EXERCISE

Time Tracking

This time-tracking exercise will allow you to see how closely your perceptions match your weekly reality. Use the following chart to record your use of time over 1 week. Take a few moments every 4 hours that you are awake and write down what you have been doing during the last 4 hours. Once the week is complete, add up the amount of time you actually spent in each of the categories of time use and write them on the chart. ●

Calendar for the week of ____________________

	Sun.	Mon.	Tues.	Wed.	Thur.	Fri.	Sat.
6 A.M.							
7							
8							
9							
10							
11							
12 P.M.							
1							
2							
3							
4							
5							
6							
7							
8							
9							
10							
11							
12 A.M.							
1–5							

Time in Class _______ hours
Studying _______ hours
Work _______ hours
Commuting _______ hours
Family Time _______ hours
Volunteer Work _______ hours
Exercise _______ hours
Athletics _______ hours
Social Time with Friends _______ hours
Sleeping _______ hours
Eating _______ hours
Grooming, Dressing, Cleaning _______ hours
Fun (TV, music, dating,
computer, phone,
hobbies, shopping) _______ hours
Other _______ hours

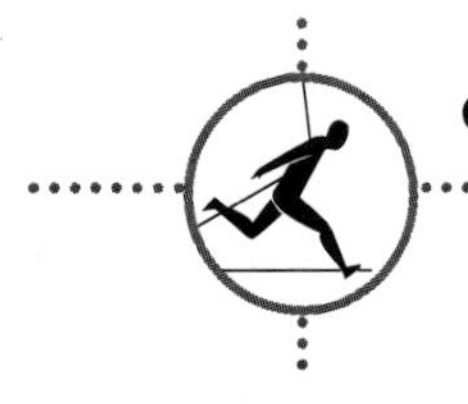

CRITICAL REFLECTION EXERCISE

How Is Your Habit?

You have drawn a picture of your time-management habits. Reflect on that picture. Talk it over with a friend or teacher who successfully manages their time. Then write out three positive things you see in your habits. Also write out the three things most in need of improvement. ●

Looks Good!

1. ______________________________
2. ______________________________
3. ______________________________

Needs Improvement!

1. ______________________________
2. ______________________________
3. ______________________________

Building a Better Time Plan

Now that you have had a chance to reflect on your time use, you can build a healthier habit. Review the goals you established for yourself in the previous chapter. Those goals will be addressed at every level in your time plan. A healthy time plan has at least three levels: the semester plan, the weekly plan, and the daily plan.

The Semester Plan

Not every week of your semester looks the same. One week you may have a paper due. Another week you may have two exams. Perhaps your best friend is getting married in April. Look for those more unique occurrences this semester and place them on a calendar. Then carefully review all course syllabi for exams, papers, and presentations. Once you have placed everything on the calendar, you may want to color code them by class or type for easy reference. A typical month might look like this.

February

Sun.	Mon.	Tues.	Wed.	Thur.	Fri.	Sat.
			1 History Exam	2	3	4
5	6	7 Second Speech	8	9	10 Sociology Paper	11
12	13	14 Dad's Birthday	15	16	17	18 Winter Festival
19	20	21	22 Club Meeting	23	24	25 Pat's Wedding
26	27 English Paper	28				

EXERCISE

Build a Semester Plan

Now it is time to build your own semester plan. Get a calendar with room to write. Then take your personal calendar, syllabi, and meeting or game schedules in hand so that you can mark the important dates. ●

The Weekly Plan

The weekly plan is designed to help you organize the regular components of your week like studying, socializing, attending class, or going to a tutoring session. By being more intentional about the time you spend doing these things, you will be more likely to find the balance you are seeking in your weekly schedule.

Study time is critical. Most college teachers expect you to put in between 1 and 2 hours of studying per week for each hour you are in class. Plan at least a portion of that study time for the daylight hours. Research has shown that work during daylight hours tends to be more productive than work done at night. But you know better than anyone else when your "prime time" occurs. That is the time during the day or week when you know you are at your best. Be sure to exploit that time for studying.

While preparing this new habit for yourself, don't view the plan as enslaving. Remember that making a schedule is creating a guide for your habits. Be ready to edit your plan if necessary. At a minimum, you will want to reevaluate your weekly time plan at midterm. Look at the following example. Then prepare a weekly schedule in the blank grid.

	Sun.	Mon.	Tues.	Wed.	Thur.	Fri.	Sat.
6 A.M.			Breakfast		Breakfast		Sleep
7		Breakfast	Study	Breakfast	Study	Breakfast	↓
8	Breakfast	History		History		History	Breakfast
9		Study	↓	Study	↓		Exercise
10			Speech		Speech		Study
11	Laundry	↓		↓			
12 P.M.	Lunch	Lunch	Lunch	Lunch	Lunch	Lunch	↓
1	Fun		Study		Study		Lunch
2							Family
3		Psych.	↓	Psych.	↓	Psych.	
4	↓		Exercise		Exercise		↓
5	Dinner	Dinner	Dinner	Dinner	Dinner	Dinner	Dinner
6	Work		Math	Work		Fun	Family
7		Tutoring			Tutoring		
8		Study	↓		Study		
9							
10		↓			↓		↓
11	↓			↓			
12 A.M.	Sleep	Sleep	Sleep	Sleep	Sleep	↓	Sleep
1–5	↓	↓	↓	↓	↓	Sleep ↓	↓

PhotoDisc/gettyimages, 2002

EXERCISE

Build a Weekly Plan

Using the blank grid on the following page, first enter the fixed elements of your week. Put in things like your class schedule, work, commuting, and practice time. Then, using a pencil (because you will need to erase!), begin to enter the more flexible parts of your day.

Now you need to enter the more flexible portions of your typical week. Go back to the time-tracking exercise and see how many hours per week you are investing in things like social time, exercising, and fun. Do you need to increase the amount of time you are spending in some areas? Do you need to decrease the amount of time you are spending in other areas? Can you work out your schedule so that you are doing two things at once, like doing laundry and reading your history assignment? ●

	Sun.	Mon.	Tues.	Wed.	Thur.	Fri.	Sat.
6 A.M.							
7							
8							
9							
10							
11							
12 P.M.							
1							
2							
3							
4							
5							
6							
7							
8							
9							
10							
11							
12 A.M.							
1–5							

The Daily Plan

The third part of building a better time plan means creating a daily list of things you plan to do. Each day will look a little different. We know that you have various ways of filling in the study time, social time, volunteer time, or fun time blocked out on your weekly calendar. You can blend those options together with your semester plan on this list. Remember the goals you have for your life. Do something every day that moves you closer to reaching those goals. For example, studying for your history exam will help you reach both your GPA goal and your goal to graduate from college.

Of course, not everything on your list will be of the same importance. That is why it is helpful to divide your list into categories of importance. You can prioritize that list by thinking in terms of things that are critical, important, and possible. Give the highest quality time to critical items, and fill in the possible items only when you have extra time. A typical daily plan may look like this.

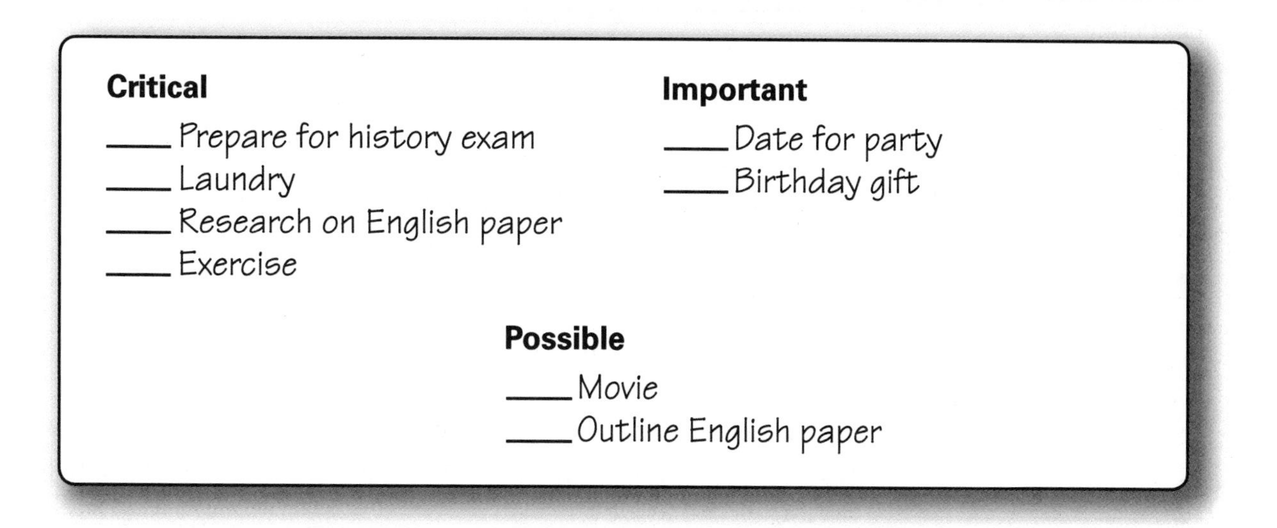

EXERCISE

Build a Daily Plan

For the next 5 days, build a daily list of things you want to accomplish. Be sure to divide that list into objectives that are critical, important, and possible. Copy the grid that follows or make up your own. ●

Today's Plan

Date: ____________________

Critical	**Important**
___ ______________________	___ ______________________
___ ______________________	___ ______________________
___ ______________________	___ ______________________
___ ______________________	___ ______________________

Possible

___ ______________________

___ ______________________

___ ______________________

Distractions and Procrastination

Distractions

We need to make one last stop in our review of your time habit. Your careful planning may be undone if you are victimized by either distractions or procrastination. Distractions come in all shapes and sizes. You may be distracted by your friends' music down the hall, by a phone call from your family, by the memory of something that happened earlier in the day, or by your own physical exhaustion. What can you do to avoid being distracted?

Some of the distractions you face come from the environment in which you are trying to work. One way to minimize these distractions is to have a specific place set aside to study. When you discipline yourself to study in the same location, your body and mind become conditioned to that space and actually move into the study mode more quickly and attentively. That environment should be comfortable, well lighted, and away from sounds, sights, and memories that may distract you.

Your friends may also distract you from accomplishing your goals with invitations and conversations that invade the time you have set aside to work. The reality is that you are responsible for controlling the way you use your time. Either you will control it or someone else will. Since you know best what goals you want to accomplish, learn to say "no" to your friends when their invitations or conversations prevent you from following your plan.

Finally, old habits can be a distraction. Maybe you are in the habit of doing most of your studying at night after a full day of work and play. Perhaps you are in the habit of studying with music or in front of the TV. Maybe you find yourself surfing the Net for fun whenever you are using your computer to write a paper. One way to identify and eliminate these kinds of distractions is by making a "not-to-do" list. Make a list of habits you wish to avoid and post it in your study environment. This list will help you change the habits you want to change so that you can be more successful.

Procrastination

Do you struggle with procrastination? Procrastination is the postponing of tasks that are perceived as unpleasant. Your procrastination may be caused by a number of factors working in isolation or in combination with one another. Put a checkmark by the items that cause you to procrastinate.

- ☐ I am not confident.
- ☐ I am easily frustrated.
- ☐ I am not motivated.
- ☐ I am bored.
- ☐ I have difficulty starting a task.
- ☐ I feel overwhelmed by this project.
- ☐ I think the task will take less time than it actually does.

Lack of confidence and frustration can be both a cause and a symptom of procrastination. One way to rebuild your confidence and defeat your frustration is to begin with a smaller task that you know you will achieve. That success will build momentum and help you break the procrastination cycle.

You may have difficulty beginning a project because you lack motivation or feel bored. If that is the case for you, check out the motivation discussion and Picture Your Motivation exercise in Chapter Three.

Remember that you can ask a friend, a teacher, or a relative to help hold you accountable for tasks you are committed to completing. Plan to reward yourself and to celebrate when you accomplish a task.

Sometimes people have difficulty starting a task because they are waiting for just the right moment to begin. But in reality, there is no magic moment. When you are tempted to delay the start of a project, make yourself sit down for 10 minutes and work on the project. After 10 minutes, decide whether or not to continue. More often than not, the momentum you build during the first 10 minutes will break the inertia and move you forward. As you get started, be aware of escape routes you have used in the past that have contributed to the delay. Don't let the habit of taking a nap, cleaning, or watching TV prevent you from getting started.

Perhaps you find yourself easily overwhelmed by the size and complexity of an assignment. But like the builder of a house, you don't do everything at once. First the builder lays the foundation, and then the frame of the house is erected. Electrical and plumbing components are added, and then the finishing work is done. When facing a big task, look for ways to break it down into small parts that you can manage and complete.

On the other hand, you might underestimate the size and complexity of an assignment. Consequently, you miscalculate the amount of time needed to complete a task and delay starting the work. If you don't catch this miscalculation early, you will be rushed to get the assignment in on time or face the consequences of handing in late work. In either case, you will likely receive a lower grade than what you could have earned. You can address this problem by setting an earlier starting date for the project. Of course, you may finish the assignment before it is due, but there is no penalty for completing a project early.

The way you use your time is a habit. This chapter has given you the opportunity to reflect on that habit. The best time managers organize the use of their time, limit distractions, and avoid procrastination. Now you are on the edge of successful time management.

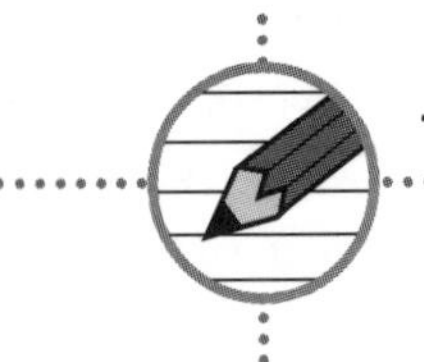

JOURNAL

You have had the opportunity to do a variety of exercises in this chapter. Write about your experiences with those exercises. What did you discover about yourself? What portions of your time-management habit do you intend to change? What will you do to bring about those changes? ●

ON THE NET

Go to Your College Success Resource Center at www.success.wadsworth.com. Click on "Discipline Resources," then look at the "Resource Web Links." There you will find a variety of links under "Time Management" that will lead you to Internet resources that will further enhance your time-management skills. You can also find additional resources and exercises for *On the Edge of Success* at http://info.wadsworth.com/clason. ●

5

Make the Most of Your Resources

What resources does my campus offer to support my success?

How can I relate more effectively to the professors who teach my classes?

Few things are more frustrating than trying to accomplish a task without having the proper tools for the job. It may have happened to you on a busy highway. You heard a bang and then felt the sad slapping of a flat tire on the pavement. You had a lug wrench to remove the flat tire. You had a spare tire full of air. But what you couldn't find anywhere in the trunk was the jack to lift your car. You know that you could successfully change the tire if you only had the right tool for the job.

The same is true for someone seeking to repair their grade point average. Like the flat tire, your GPA is reparable as long as you have the right tools for the job. The good news is that your school has provided you with tools and resources that will help you do just that. This chapter is about discovering the tools that your school has in place to help you reach your goals.

Your School's Resources

Your school wants you to be successful. That is why it provides services like tutoring, healthcare, and financial aid. Here is a list of resources that many schools provide.

Teaching faculty

Teaching assistants

Residence hall staff

Academic advisors
Academic tutors
Writing centers
Study groups
Math labs
Career center
Computer labs
Library
Counseling center
Disability services
Financial aid office
Minority student center
Health services

EXERCISE

Discover the Resources on Your Campus

The first step is to discover what resources are most likely to help you at the moment. Consult the student handbook, your school's Web page, your advisor, or the advising center to learn what resources are offered at your school. From that larger list, identify the six resources that will make the greatest contribution to your climb up the pyramid of success. Collect all the vital information on these resources and list them in the box on the following page.

Just knowing that these resources exist will not be helpful unless you put them to work during your week. If these resources are going to become a meaningful part of your success strategy, then you will have to incorporate them into the time-management plan you developed in the previous chapter. For example, if you believe tutoring will help you reach your grade goal in history class, then you need to set aside time each week for a session with your tutor. ●

Your School's Faculty

The professionals who have been given the greatest responsibility for your intellectual growth are the faculty members who teach your classes. College teachers are different from other teachers you have

Key Resources

Resource	Contact Person	Phone Number	E-Mail Address	Web Page	Hours	Location

had both in their professional life and in the way they present their classes. They have advanced academic degrees in specialties like history, English, or biology. They see themselves not only as teachers but also as experts in their specialty area. Thus, they spend time writing books and articles as well as speaking publicly on their area of expertise.

The classes they conduct ask more of you. The faculty assign more reading over less time and give you exams on that reading even if they have not discussed that material in class. They ask you to be more responsible as a student. They are less likely to check up on either your class attendance or note taking. They expect that you will know when assignments are due and what percentage of the grade each assignment and test is worth.

They are less tolerant of simple answers to complex questions. They invite class members to engage in robust discussion that encourages a variety of opinions to be heard and evaluated. You can expect them to be sympathetic to personal challenges you face while holding you to high academic standards.

CRITICAL THINKING EXERCISE

Your Favorite Kind of Teacher

College teachers are different from other teachers you have had, but this does not mean they are all the same. If you were to visit a number of classes being taught on your campus, you would find faculty with a variety of personalities and presentation styles. Not everyone likes the same kind of teacher. This exercise will help you find the qualities that are important to you as a learner. It will create a picture of your favorite teacher.

Pick a favorite teacher in whose class you really learned a lot. Assess that instructor according to the criteria that follow. The teacher will be stronger in some areas and weaker in others. Put an X on the continuum to indicate the relative strength or weakness of that teacher. The last two lines are blank so that you can add important qualities we may have missed.

Using this information, answer the following questions:

1. What qualities does this teacher have that helped you learn more easily?
2. Since you may have the option of taking a college class from more than one instructor, what three qualities will be most important to you in making that choice? •

Knows the subject well

Weak ________________________________ Strong

Keeps my attention

Weak ________________________________ Strong

Is organized

Weak ________________________________ Strong

Stops and starts class on time

Weak ________________________________ Strong

Is approachable

Weak ________________________________ Strong

Has a sense of humor

Weak ________________________________ Strong

Grades fairly

Weak ________________________________ Strong

Is available for meetings

Weak ________________________________ Strong

Weak ________________________________ Strong

Weak ________________________________ Strong

PhotoDisc/gettyimages, 2002

Tips for Relating to Your Teachers

The relationship you have with your teachers plays an important role in your college success. Successful students understand this and have offered the following advice when interacting with college teachers.

Show them that you are serious about your work by doing it.

Attend class and arrive on time.

Be courteous and respectful.

Don't sleep in class.

Hand in all work on time.

Avoid the regular use of excuses.

Sit in the front of the room.

Remember that teachers are people too!

EXERCISE

Keep in Touch

Good communication with your instructors is essential to your climb up the pyramid of success. Most instructors have time set aside weekly during which they meet with their students. Take advantage of this time or set up an appointment to see each of your instructors once every 4 to 5 weeks during the semester. Ask questions such as the following:

What is my current grade?

What am I doing well in your class?

What can I do to be more successful in your class? ●

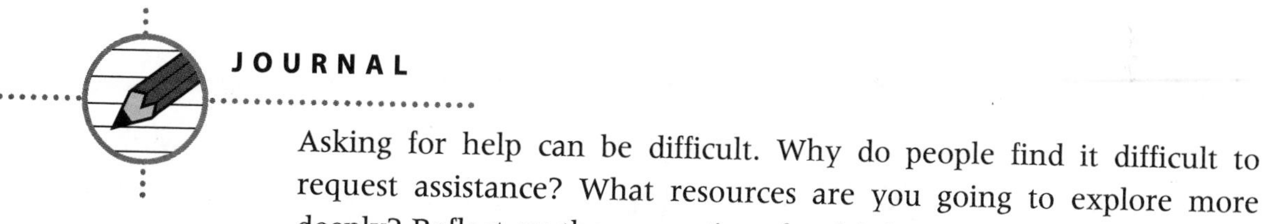

JOURNAL

Asking for help can be difficult. Why do people find it difficult to request assistance? What resources are you going to explore more deeply? Reflect on these questions for this journal entry. ●

ON THE NET

Go to www.success.wadsworth.com. Click on "Discipline Resources" and then on "Study Skills/Strategies." There you will find several pages that will enhance your ability to work with college faculty. Check out "Choosing Teachers" and "Student to Teacher Etiquette." If your school has an academic Web page, surf it for information about other resources offered on your campus. You can also find additional resources and exercises for *On the Edge of Success* at http://info.wadsworth.com/clason. ●

6

Learn about Your Learning Style

What is my preferred learning style?

How can I learn more efficiently?

How do you like to learn? Whether you know it or not, you have a preferred learning style. Preferences make us unique and influence our daily habits and lifestyle choices. You have a preference for certain foods, styles of clothing, and a preference for which hand you use to write. Your preferences can influence how and where you live. Do you prefer the city, the suburbs, or a farm? Do you prefer the beach or the mountains? Do you want to live in a climate that is warm year-round or do you like seasonal changes? These preferences are unlikely to influence your academic success. But there are *learning style* preferences that greatly affect your academic potential. Understanding these will impact the way you climb the pyramid of success.

Imagine that you have just purchased a vacuum cleaner. You bring it home and need to assemble the vacuum cleaner before it can be used. You open the box and remove the contents. What would be your next move? Check the box that describes your most likely course of action.

- ❑ I would read and follow the written instructions.
- ❑ I would study the diagrams within the instructions and look at the picture on the box.
- ❑ I would pick up each of the pieces and assemble them by trial and error.

Although you may use all these techniques at some point in the assembly, chances are you have a certain preference for the way you would complete this task.

The way you prefer to assemble a vacuum cleaner begins to reveal your preferences for learning. This chapter will help you discover and apply your preferred style of learning. Successful students know their learning style and know how to use it to their advantage both in and out of the classroom. You may be working very hard to succeed in a class but failing in your efforts because you are not using your natural preference for learning. You will discover that there are different styles of learning. It is important for you to know from the start that there is no single style of learning that is better than another. As long as the vacuum cleaner runs smoothly and picks up dirt, it doesn't really matter how you assembled it!

CRITICAL REFLECTION EXERCISE

Initial Impressions of Your Learning Style

A learning style is your preferred way of obtaining and sharing knowledge. Each of us has a preferred learning style. That learning style difference may become apparent in the type of test you prefer to take. Would you rather take a multiple-choice test or an essay test? Why? In the following box, explain your choice in two or three sentences. ●

Your answer gives you important clues to your preferred method of learning. If you prefer multiple-choice tests (or similar types), you probably feel more comfortable dealing with the world of facts and concrete examples. If you like essay tests, you may prefer dealing with theories and abstract ideas rather than facts. It is essential that you discover your learning style because this preference impacts how you study for tests. If a multiple-choice exam tests your knowledge of facts, and you have studied the information to understand theories and ideas, you may have missed important information. If you study for an essay test by learning only the detailed facts, you may have missed the larger picture of theories and abstract thoughts.

If you have not thought about your learning style before, this preview has given you a good start. But there are also more formal methods of discovering your learning style that we will pursue in the next section.

Verbal, Visual, and Kinesthetic Learning

How did you put together the vacuum cleaner? There are many ways to assess your learning style, but one way is to consider whether you are a more verbal, visual, or kinesthetic learner. As in the example with the vacuum cleaner, you probably use all three at some time, but it is likely that you are stronger in one area. Look at the following lists for each type of learner. Check the statements that best describe you.

Verbal

- ❑ I usually remember what I read or write down.
- ❑ I can remember more easily what my instructor says.
- ❑ I would rather call someone on the phone than write a letter.
- ❑ I like talking about interesting topics.
- ❑ I would read the directions when assembling a vacuum cleaner.

Visual

- ❑ I usually learn more from diagrams, maps, charts, and pictures.
- ❑ I would rather have a map than written directions.
- ❑ I usually remember what my instructor writes on the board.
- ❑ I like textbooks with lots of colors and pictures.
- ❑ I would rely on the diagrams to assemble a vacuum cleaner.

Kinesthetic

- ❑ I like working with my hands.
- ❑ I enjoy classes that have a lab.
- ❑ I like teachers who move about the room instead of sitting or standing.
- ❑ I would assemble the vacuum cleaner by trial and error—putting the pieces together that seem to fit.

This exercise will help you discover your learning preferences. Your approach to learning may be more balanced or may favor one preference. Which description sounds most like you? Read the following suggestions to see how you may improve your study skills.

Verbal Learners

Verbal learners usually learn better with written or spoken language. If you believe you are stronger in the verbal area, here are things you can do to help you study.

- Rewrite your notes.
- Outline reading material.
- Recite your notes out loud.
- Discuss the class material with another person.
- Rewrite your class notes while adding notes from the textbooks.

Visual Learners

Visual learners usually learn better with information presented visually, as in pictures or images. If you believe you are stronger in the visual area, here are things you can do to help you study.

- Examine the diagrams and charts in your textbooks.
- Rewrite your notes using mind maps and time lines.
- Highlight your notes or textbooks with different colors.
- Color code with highlighters (e.g., yellow for facts; blue for definitions).
- Lay out your notes on your desk to study them and visualize the location of information on your desktop when taking an exam.

Kinesthetic Learners

Kinesthetic learners usually learn better when they are moving or doing something active. If you believe you are stronger in the kinesthetic area, here are things you can do to help you study.

Box 6.1

"Professor Smith Is Driving Me Crazy..."

Do you find yourself frustrated in a class and don't know why? Maybe your instructor's teaching style is at odds with your learning style. Instructors have a tendency to teach the way they learn. If you are a visual learner in a class with an instructor who only lectures and discusses, you probably feel a bit frustrated. At times like these, it is critical to use the techniques of your learning style to study the material. Find a student in the class who is having similar difficulties. Together, you may be able to help each other "translate" all the verbal information into a visual format that is easier for you to grasp. Also, talk to students who are doing well in the class and ask them how they take notes and study for the exams. They may be able to give you valuable tips you may not think of yourself.

- Recite your notes out loud while pacing or moving about your room.
- Create flashcards.
- Teach or present the material you are studying to a friend.
- Draw mind maps or pictures to accompany your notes.

Try the suggestions that fit your learning style preference. If you are a visual learner, use the visual techniques to study. But remember that this is only a preference. Don't hesitate to experiment with some of the other suggestions. Try using some verbal and kinesthetic learning techniques to supplement your dominant preference.

Learning Styles Exploration

You may also explore your learning style by studying the personality types described in the work of Isabel Briggs Myers and Katharine Myers.[1] They developed a personality inventory based on Carl Jung's theory of psychological types. It explores four aspects of personality preferences. The following exercise is based on these personality preferences as they relate to learning styles. This is not an intelligence test. Thus, you will not receive a grade. The exercise is designed to illuminate your personality preferences. You will discover things like

1. Myers, Isabel Briggs (with P. B. Myers). (1980). *Gifts differing: Understanding personality type.* Palo Alto, CA: Davies-Black.

PhotoDisc/gettyimages, 2002

whether you prefer to work in groups or individually, whether you like to make decisions based on facts or feelings, and whether you prefer to plan or be spontaneous.

CRITICAL REFLECTION EXERCISE

Explore Your Learning Style

Extrovert/Introvert

This preference reveals where people like to focus their energy and attention.

Extroverted people like to focus their energy on the outer world of people and activities. Are you outgoing and talkative? Do you like working with people? Do you feel energized at a party? Do you like to relax by talking with a group of friends? If you have a problem, are you most likely to "talk it out" with a trusted friend? Then you are probably an extrovert. Extroverts focus on the world around them and like to interact with the people in that world.

Introverted people like to focus their energy on the inner world of thoughts and ideas. Do you enjoy quiet times and relaxing by yourself? Are you more likely to ponder and think through a problem than discuss it? Do you prefer to work alone rather than in a group? Are you bothered by interruptions? If so, you may be an introvert. Although introverts certainly like people, they usually prefer to work or study quietly by themselves.

You are likely to be a blend of both introversion and extroversion, but one of these two preferences will be stronger than the other. Estimate what percentage of your personality is more extroverted and what percentage is more introverted. Combined they should total 100 percent.

Extroverted (E) ___40___%

Introverted (I) ___60___%

On the left side of the circle that follows, place either an E or I to reflect the higher percentage you have indicated. Place that percentage value in the lower right segment of the circle.

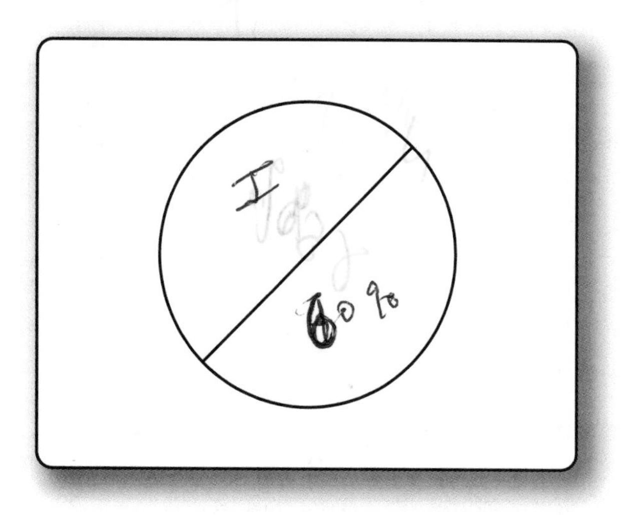

Sensing/Intuitive

This scale expresses your preference for acquiring information.

Sensing people like to work with the facts that they have obtained from their five senses. Do you prefer to deal with present and concrete information like facts and figures? Do you see yourself as practical? Are you good with details? Are you realistic? If so, you are probably a sensing individual. Sensing people can engage in theoretical discussion; however, they prefer the world of facts.

Intuitive people prefer to deal with the world of ideas. Do you enjoy a discussion about an abstract philosophical concept or theory? Do you move quickly from the bare facts to their relationship to one another? Do you tend to look for the "big picture" and not notice the details? Do you have a tendency to think ahead into future possibilities? You might be an intuitive person. Intuitive types understand details and facts but prefer to find the relationships and meaning between the facts.

You are likely to be both sensing and intuitive, but one of these two preferences will be stronger than the other. Estimate what percentage of your personality is more sensing and what percentage is more intuitive. Combined they should total 100 percent.

Sensing (S) __15__%
Intuitive (N) __85__%

On the left side of the circle that follows, place either an S or N to reflect the higher percentage you have indicated. Place that percentage value in the lower right segment of the circle.

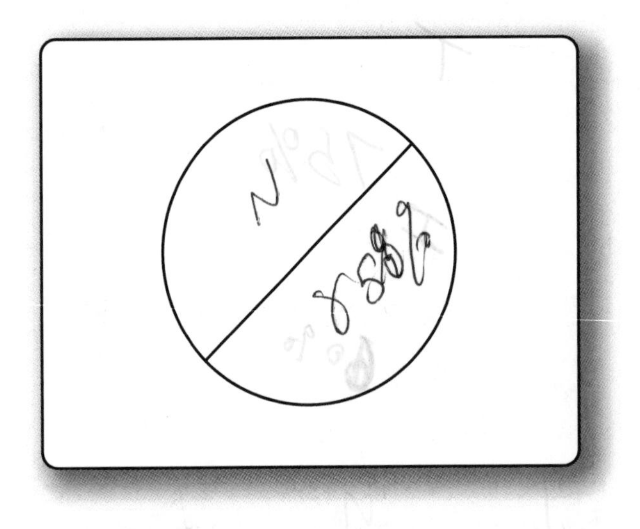

Thinking/Feeling

This scale reveals your preference for making decisions.

Thinkers prefer to make decisions based on logical analysis. Do you usually make decisions after carefully collecting and weighing all the facts? Do you try to remain objective when making a decision? If so, you are probably a thinker. Thinkers obviously have emotions and feelings like everyone else. They just prefer making decisions based on facts and evidence.

Feelers prefer to make decisions by considering values and emotions. Do you usually make decisions based on how you feel or how others may be impacted emotionally by your decision? Do you try to maintain harmony with those around you? If so, you are probably a feeler. Feelers take into account the logic and facts of a decision. However, the facts are secondary in consideration to feelings and personal values.

You are likely to be a blend of both the thinker and the feeler, but one of these two preferences will be stronger than the other. Estimate what percentage of your personality is more the thinker and what percentage is more the feeler. Combined they should total 100 percent.

Thinking (T) 75 %
Feeling (F) 25 %

On the left side of the circle that follows, place either a T or F to reflect the higher percentage you have indicated. Place that percentage value in the lower right segment of the circle.

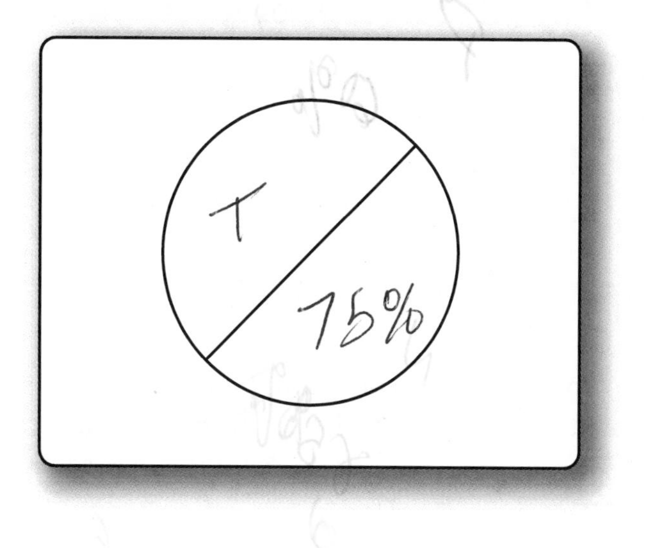

Judging/Perceiving

This scale reveals your preference for planning your life.

Judgers like plans and organization. Do you prefer structure to your day and week? Do you like organizing information and making concrete plans? Do you set goals and try to stick to them? Do you make lists of things to do? Do you have daily and weekly plans? Do you have a calendar that keeps track of your assignments? Do you complete the tasks you begin? Judgers like to live in an orderly world.

Perceivers like flexibility and spontaneity. Do you like to experience life without feeling the need to plan your day? Do you go with the flow? Do you put off decisions while you continue to gather information? Do you struggle with procrastination? Do you see yourself as flexible? Do you find it easy to leave tasks uncompleted? Perceivers feel too constrained living by a daily or weekly plan.

You are likely to be both judging and perceiving, but one of these two preferences will be stronger than the other. Estimate what percentage of your personality is more judging and what percentage is more perceiving. Combined they should total 100 percent.

Judging (J) __40__%

Perceiving (P) __60__%

On the left side of the circle that follows, place either a J or P to reflect the higher percentage you have indicated. Place that percentage value in the lower right segment of the circle.

Now it is time to bring this information together. Collect the letters from the four circles and enter each letter on these lines.

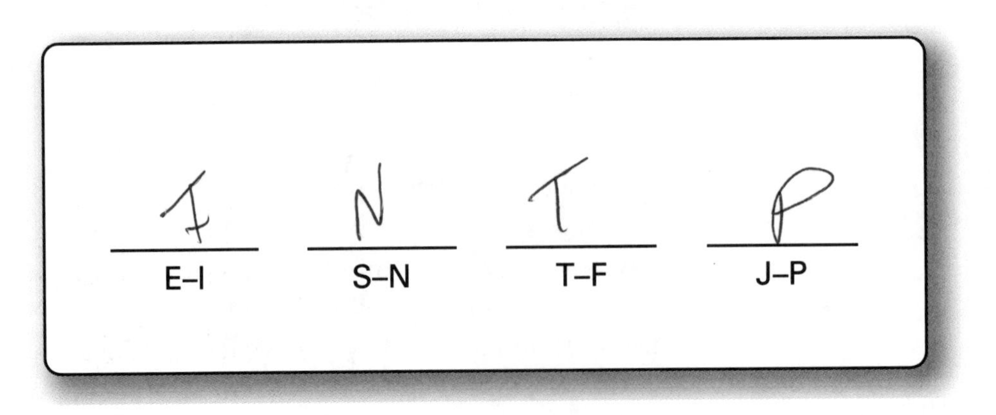

This is how you see yourself at the moment. No personality is without strengths and weaknesses. Let's look at how your preferences impact the success of your learning. Check the following list for possible strengths and weaknesses of your personality type. ●

Strengths and Weaknesses of the Types

	Possible Strengths	Possible Weaknesses
Introvert	is independent works alone reflects works with ideas avoids generalizations is careful before acting	avoids others is secretive loses opportunities to act is misunderstood by others dislikes being interrupted
Extrovert	interacts with others is open acts, does is well understood	needs people to work needs change and variety is impulsive is impatient with routine
Intuitor	sees possibilities works out new ideas works with the complicated solves novel problems	is inattentive to detail is inattentive to practical is impatient with the tedious loses sight of here and now jumps to conclusions
Sensor	attends to detail is practical has memory for details/facts is patient is systematic	does not see possibilities loses the overall in details mistrusts intuition is frustrated with complicated prefers not to imagine future
Feeler	considers others' feelings understands needs, values is interested in conciliation demonstrates feelings persuades, arouses	is not guided by logic is not objective is less organized is overly accepting
Thinker	is logical and analytical is objective is organized has critical ability is just stands firm	may not notice others' feelings misunderstands others' values is uninterested in conciliation does not show feelings shows less compassion
Perceiver	compromises sees all sides of issues is flexible decides based only on data is not judgmental	is indecisive does not plan does not control circumstances is easily distracted from tasks does not finish projects
Judger	decides plans orders makes quick decisions remains with a task	is stubborn is inflexible decides with insufficient data is controlled by task or plans wishes not to interrupt work

Adapted from Gardner, J. N. & Jewler, A. J. (2000). *Your College Experience: Strategies for Success.* Belmont, CA: Wadsworth, pp. 71–72.

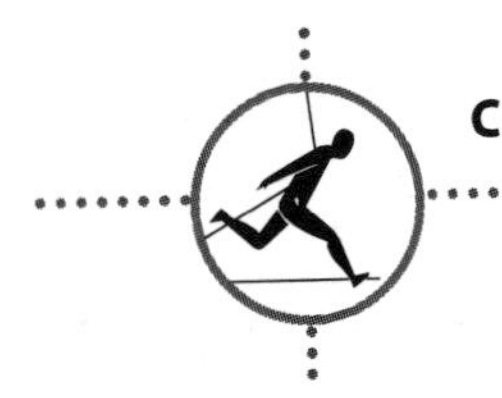

CRITICAL THINKING EXERCISE

Apply Your Learning Style

Throughout this chapter, you have been gathering information about your learning style and your personality preferences. It is now time to put that information to work. First, using the material from the previous exercise, describe your personality preferences and how that impacts your learning style.

My personality type is . . .

____

____

Because of my type, I believe my greatest strengths are . . .

____

____

Because of my type, I believe my greatest weaknesses are . . .

____

____

Now that you are more aware of your own personality profile, see if you can guess the personality style of your instructor. Check out the syllabus and the classroom presentations of your teacher. Is this instructor more introverted or extroverted, sensing or intuitive, feeling or thinking, judging or perceiving? Many students find that they are able to learn more easily from an instructor whose personality style is similar to their own. Do you find that to be true?

Let's consider a different class. How has the instructor designed the class? Does the instructor's presentation favor a visual, verbal, or kinesthetic learner? Is it a class that deals with facts and figures or is it more theoretically oriented? If it contains elements of both, does one outweigh the other? Do the exams favor the sensor or the intuitor? If you have not yet had a test, ask other students who already took the class. Or better yet, ask the instructor what kinds of tests you can expect. Then, write out three specific techniques that you can use when studying for the tests. Keep in mind both your learning styles and the nature of the class.

Class: ____________________

Which learning style(s) does the instructor's presentation favor?

____

Which learning style(s) do the instructor's examinations favor?

____

Because of the nature of this class, I plan to use the following techniques:

1. ____________________

2. ____________________

3. ____________________

Remember, no one knows better how you learn than you. Successful students are aware of their learning preferences and use that knowledge to become more powerful learners. Now you are on the edge of successful learning by knowing your learning style preferences. ●

JOURNAL

What kind of learner are you? Write a summary of what you have discovered about your learning style after completing the exercises in this chapter. How do you plan to use that information to be a more successful student? ●

ON THE NET

If you would like to sample a learning inventory, try the Keirsey Temperament Sorter at http://www.keirsey.com. Go to "The Keirsey Character Sorter" link. Another learning style inventory is available at www.ttuhsc.edu/success/LSTIntro.htm. Here you will meet The Success Types Learning Style Type Indicator. More information on learning styles may also be found at Wadsworth's Your College Success Resource Center. Go to www.success.wadsworth.com. Click on "Discipline Resources" and then on "Resource Web Links." You can also find additional resources and exercises for *On the Edge of Success* at http://info.wadsworth.com/clason. ●

7

Read to Remember

Do you spend a lot of time reading a textbook such as this? You should. Let's do the math together and discover why. Most college students are assigned over 2000 pages of reading each semester. On average, that means you will be reading between 75 and 150 pages of history, literature, science, and English every week. This is why we are not surprised when college students report they spend more than 75 percent of their homework time reading. If you are a strong reader, that is great news. If you have difficulty with attentiveness or comprehension when you read, this part of college life can really challenge you.

This chapter will help you find strategies that can make you a better reader. Of course, there are different kinds of reading. When you read your favorite magazine, you are *reading for pleasure*. When you read directions for setting up your computer, you are reading *to immediately apply* what you read. When you carefully read the contract before purchasing your car, you are reading *to evaluate* the purchase agreement you are making. The kind of reading we are talking about here is a little different. This chapter focuses on the type of reading most commonly done by college students when they read their textbooks. They are reading *to understand and remember content.*

The strategy you used in high school for reading a textbook needs refining. College textbooks are written differently from those used in high school.

Where and when should I read?

What is intentional reading?

How can I create a record of what I am reading?

In high school, you may have used a textbook for the entire year. In college, you will most likely use a textbook for only one semester or one quarter. Although read in a shorter amount of time, college textbooks contain much more information than the average high school textbook. And college textbooks are written at a higher reading level with more difficult sentence structure and vocabulary. If you are going to climb the pyramid of success, you need strategies to help you read this kind of textbook successfully. In this chapter, we present strategies for reading in three categories: choosing the right reading environment, reading intentionally, and creating a recyclable reading record.

Where and When to Read

Have you found yourself taking "thought vacations" during your reading assignments? This frustrating loss of concentration requires that you either reread the section or sacrifice comprehension. Look through the following list and put a checkmark beside the distractions that most often victimize you when you read.

- ❑ Television
- ❑ Music
- ❑ Talking
- ❑ Temperature
- ❑ Lighting
- ❑ Uncomfortable seating
- ❑ Long reading assignment

Distractions

Choosing your reading environment carefully will help you defeat the distractions you marked. Let's talk about three ways you can improve your reading experience beginning with noise. Various types of noise can break your concentration as you read. Right in the middle of reading your history assignment you may be distracted by your neighbor's music, a TV commercial, a slamming door, or your friend's laughter. Absolute quiet may not be the solution either because that can be more distracting than normal background sounds. The goal here is to avoid sound that varies in intensity and volume.

Quiet music playing in the background may work fine for you. However, it is unlikely that you will be distraction free if you are studying with the TV or radio on. By their very nature, TV and radio change intensity and volume to recall the viewer's or listener's attention. If you have been in the habit of trying to read with the TV or radio on, try to read for a week without it and see if it makes a difference in your attentiveness.

Fatigue

Fatigue can also cause you to take thought vacations. This fatigue may be due to the time of day you are reading or the amount of time you are trying to read in one sitting. Reading your college textbook assignments belongs in the prime time of your day. That is the time of day you are most alert and attentive. Be careful that these assignments do not fall into empty, unclaimed spaces in your day when you are less alert.

You also need to pay attention to the amount of time you read in one sitting. The amount of time you read before becoming fatigued is a matter of habit. With practice, you will be able to read for 50 minutes before taking a 10-minute break. If you cannot read for 50 minutes, divide larger reading assignments into smaller and more manageable chunks. Try reading for 10 minutes without breaking. Then, keep increasing you reading time by 10-minute increments until you reach 50 minutes.

Location

Finally, be careful about your reading location. That too may distract you from your work. First, designate a specific location in your hall or library that you use for reading. This spot should not be associated with any other activity like sleep, TV, or talk time with your friends. It should be away from distracting noises. By using one spot to read, you will condition yourself into the reading mode quickly. You will also maintain a higher level of focus on your task. Be sure this location has comfortable seating and temperature as well as adequate lighting. Avoid environments where poor lighting creates shadows on your work or results in eyestrain. Careful selection of your reading environment will help eliminate your frustrating thought vacations.

Read Intentionally

Once you have established a sound reading environment, it is time to check on how *intentionally* you read. Think of reading as a shopping trip. There are two ways you can shop. You can make up a list of things

Box 7.1

Rereading Is a Habit

If you have tried to defeat all the distractions in your life by employing the suggestions under Where and When to Read, there is one more thing you can do to avoid rereading a paragraph in your textbook. Rereading can become such a habit that you do it even when it is not necessary for comprehension. The rereading habit lowers your attentiveness the first time you read a section because you know that you will be "rereading" that section soon anyway. You get in the habit of not paying attention. One way to defeat this habit is to read with a piece of paper that you slide down the page covering the sentences you have already read. By covering the sentences you have already read, you are disciplining yourself to read a sentence only once. This procedure may sound too simple to work, but it does. Try it if you want to build a more attentive reading habit.

you need and then intentionally walk from place to place in the store to get them. The alternative is more haphazard. You don't go to the store with a list of what you want to buy. You simply walk the aisles, looking here and there to see what might be of interest.

Perhaps your reading has looked more like that haphazard shopping trip. Since you don't have a "list" of what you want, your eyes wander over sentences and words without the intention of taking away meaning. You may catch yourself turning the page without being aware that you have read it. The alternative is reading with a "shopping list" in hand. When you read intentionally, you actively pursue ideas, not just words.

Preview

Here is how you read intentionally. First, you preview the contents of the chapter. This step takes no more than 5 minutes. Your car's engine will run better if you give it just a few moments to warm up. The same is true of your reading. This preview gets your reading engine warmed up and gives you a sense of the chapter's organization. Page through the chapter and note its title and any other headings. Take a moment to read the introduction and other portions of the text set off in bold, italics, or with bullets. Glance over the charts, illustrations, and pictures. At the close of this preview, you will have a sense of what the chapter is about.

PhotoDisc/gettyimages, 2002

Question

Now it is time to write down questions you want this chapter to answer for you. Write these questions on a note card, in the margin of the book itself, or on a piece of paper that is divided into recall and record columns. These questions are your shopping list! Now go to the store, read the chapter, and find the answers to your questions. Because you are reading with intention, this kind of reading will become a directed quest rather than an aimless journey.

Create a Recyclable Reading Record

Reading the chapter of a textbook takes time and energy. If you follow the plan we are suggesting, you will need to read the chapter only once. You will have created a recyclable reading record that has captured and summarized the message of the author. We will illustrate several forms that record might take. Each one preserves the answers to the questions you wrote down during the preview step. Find one that fits your style.

Answer the Questions

If you have written the questions that you wish the chapter to answer in the margin of your textbook, you may want to answer the questions by marking the paragraphs in the textbook itself. That marking may be done with a highlighter or with a pen using a system of underlining and annotating you design yourself. In either case, be sure that you read an entire paragraph or section before you begin marking the text. This allows you to find the portion of the text that best answers your questions. Too much marking is not helpful. Be selective and mark only that portion of the text that really summarizes the answer to the question you raised.

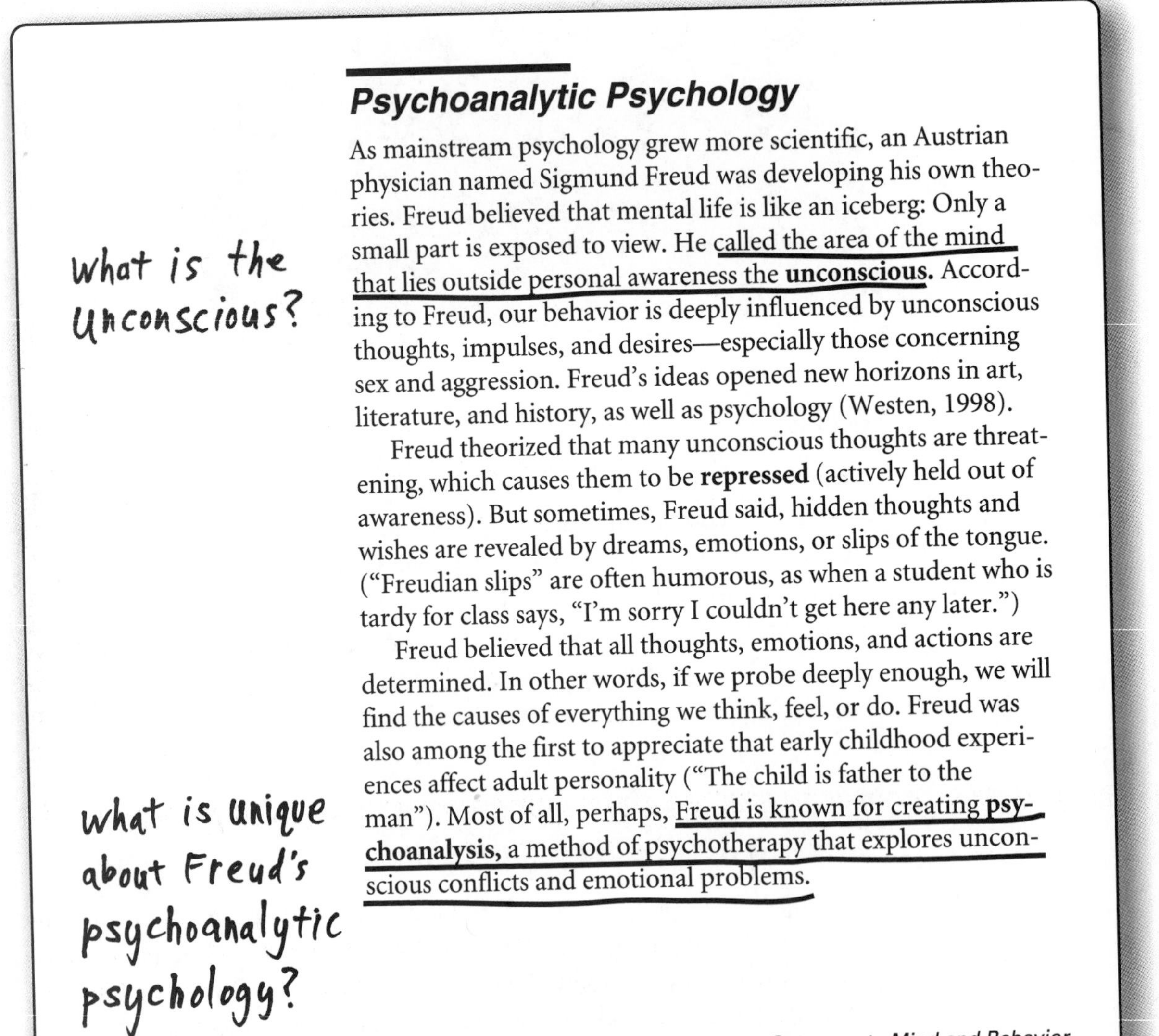

Psychoanalytic Psychology

What is the unconscious?

As mainstream psychology grew more scientific, an Austrian physician named Sigmund Freud was developing his own theories. Freud believed that mental life is like an iceberg: Only a small part is exposed to view. He called the area of the mind that lies outside personal awareness the **unconscious.** According to Freud, our behavior is deeply influenced by unconscious thoughts, impulses, and desires—especially those concerning sex and aggression. Freud's ideas opened new horizons in art, literature, and history, as well as psychology (Westen, 1998).

Freud theorized that many unconscious thoughts are threatening, which causes them to be **repressed** (actively held out of awareness). But sometimes, Freud said, hidden thoughts and wishes are revealed by dreams, emotions, or slips of the tongue. ("Freudian slips" are often humorous, as when a student who is tardy for class says, "I'm sorry I couldn't get here any later.")

What is unique about Freud's psychoanalytic psychology?

Freud believed that all thoughts, emotions, and actions are determined. In other words, if we probe deeply enough, we will find the causes of everything we think, feel, or do. Freud was also among the first to appreciate that early childhood experiences affect adult personality ("The child is father to the man"). Most of all, perhaps, Freud is known for creating **psychoanalysis,** a method of psychotherapy that explores unconscious conflicts and emotional problems.

From D. Coon, *Introduction to Psychology: Gateways to Mind and Behavior*, 9th ed. (Belmont, CA: Wadsworth, 2001), p. 12.

Another way of preserving your reading is by writing your questions and answers on note cards. Put the question on one side and the answer on the other. This creates a set of flashcards that preserves the key ideas of the chapter.

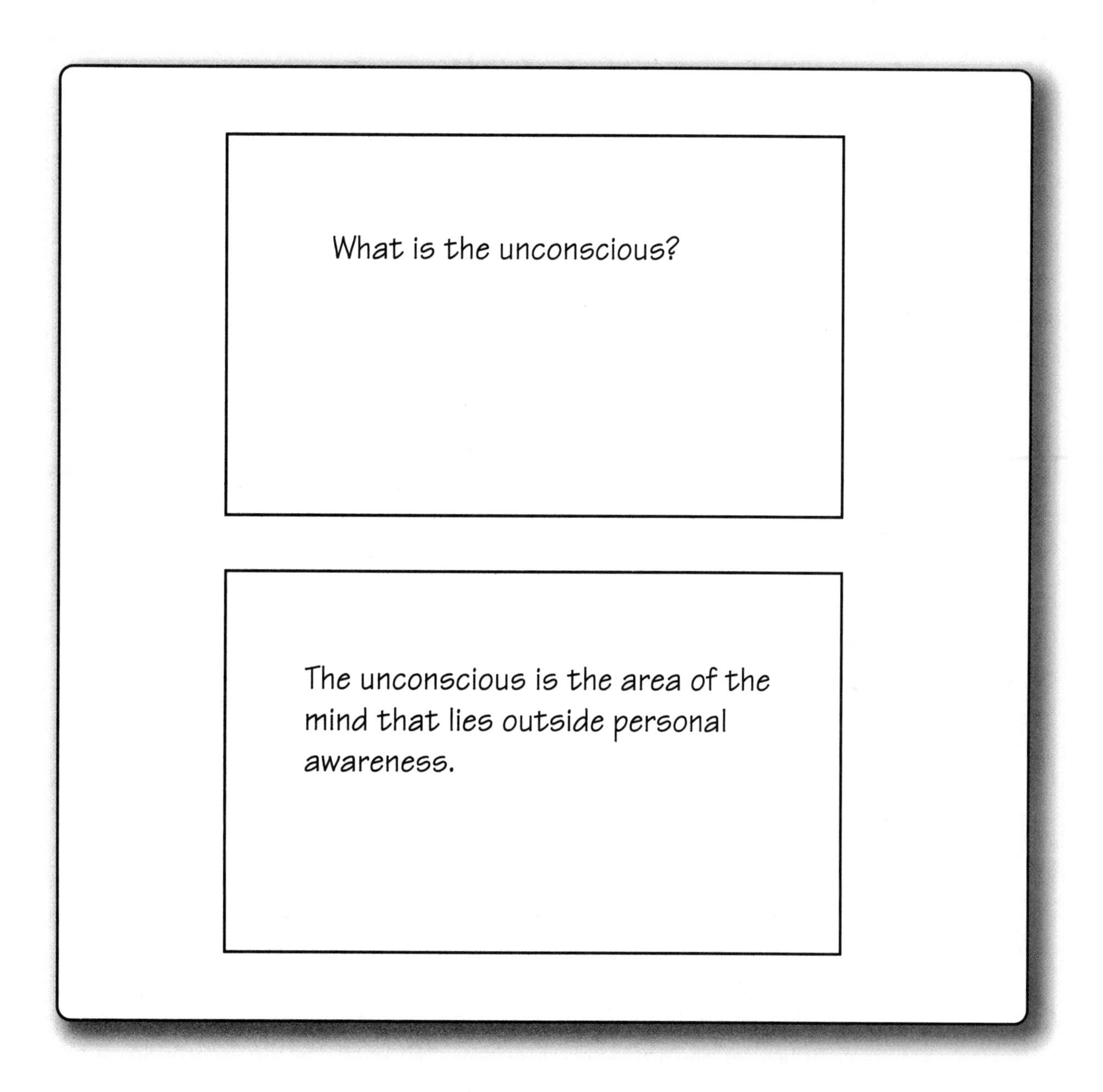

A third manner to preserve the questions and answers is on an 8 × 11 inch piece of paper that is divided into two columns. The column on the left should be narrower than the column on the right (about 3 inches). The left column is the recall column and the right column is the recording column. Put your questions on the left and the answers on the right. This will allow you to cover the record column and quiz yourself with the questions you have written in the recall column.

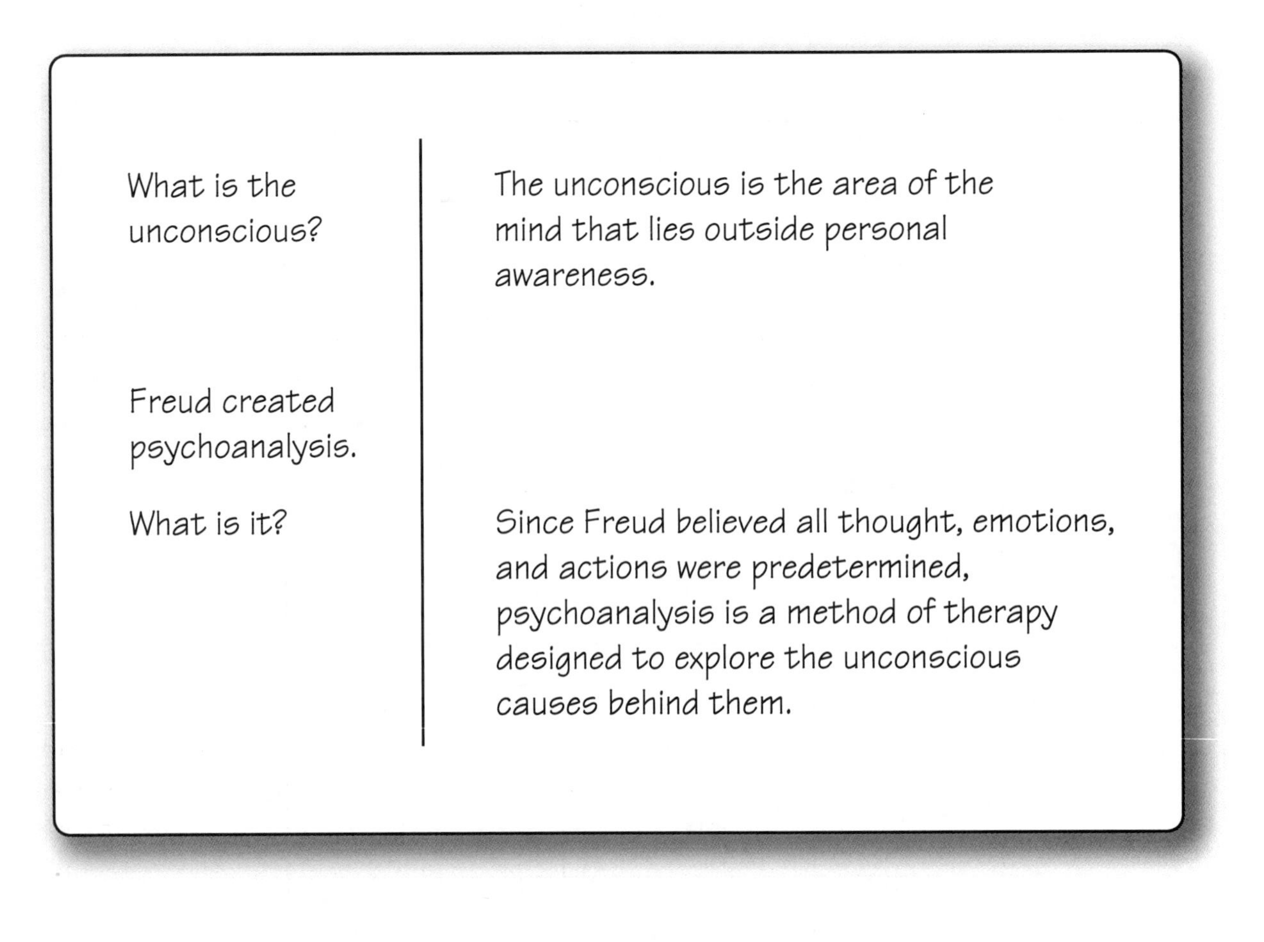

Recycle the Reading

The key to this system is not the type of recording system you use but how regularly you recycle what you have read. The process of intentional reading improves both your concentration and retention. But the real key to success here is the frequency with which you recycle those notes in review. If you spend 50 minutes reading, plan on spending at least 25 minutes after you read recycling the record. See if you can answer the questions you have raised. Look for connections between the questions and the purpose of the entire chapter. Recycle what you have read regularly and you will see your comprehension enhanced significantly.

You will be spending a significant portion of your study time reading. It is important to use this time effectively. By using the suggestions offered in this chapter, you will put yourself on the edge of successful reading.

EXERCISE

Design Your Reading System

Now that you have been introduced to an effective system of reading your textbooks, it is time to design your own system. Take the ideas that have been presented in this chapter, edit them, add your own, and develop a three-, four-, or five-step system for reading a textbook. Be sure to design something that you are willing to try. Then apply that system to your textbook reading in one of your classes. Commit yourself to experiment for 2 weeks. At the end of the second week, prepare a two-page report. First, describe the system with which you experimented. Then, based on your experiment, report on what needed to be changed. At the end of this process, you will have a personally designed system that will make you a more effective textbook reader. ●

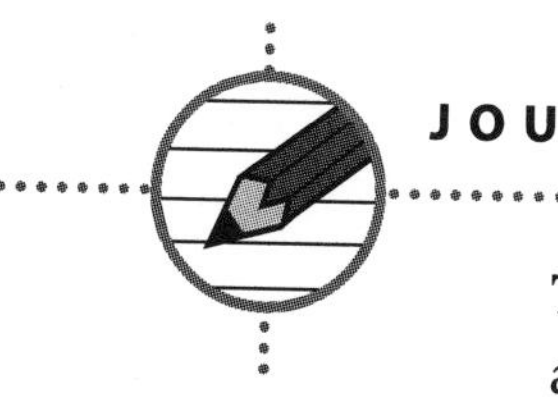

JOURNAL

This chapter has offered you advice on the time of day that you read and on the environment in which you read. Describe your own ideal reading environment taking into account all the criteria mentioned earlier. Then reflect on the time of day when you do your best reading. What habits do you need to change? ●

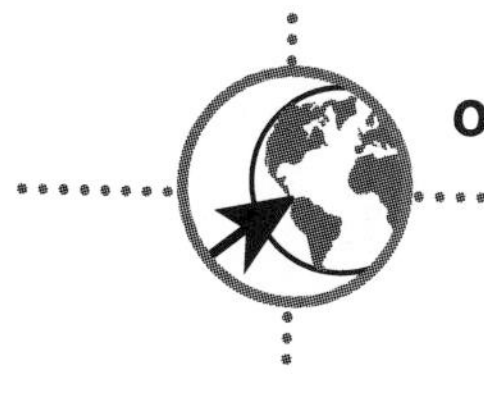

ON THE NET

You can read more about this topic of textbook reading on the Internet. Go to www.success.wadsworth.com. Click on "Discipline Resources" and then on "Resource Web Links." You can also find additional resources and exercises for *On the Edge of Success* at http://info.wadsworth.com/clason. ●

8

Take Effective Notes

Keena runs to history class and finds a seat in the back of the classroom. The lecture has already started. She struggles to find a pen or pencil in her backpack while asking the student next to her for a few sheets of paper. During the lecture, Keena tries to take notes, but she can't figure out what to write. Keena has trouble following the lecture and picking out the main points. To make matters worse, she is distracted by thoughts of her date later that evening.

After the class is over, Keena stuffs the loose sheets of paper into her backpack and quickly leaves for lunch. Later, while cleaning out her backpack, she finds her notes and places them in the folder for history class. The notes have no clear organizational pattern, are not dated, are barely legible, and the margins are filled with doodles. When the time comes to study for her history test, Keena's notes will be of little help.

Keena's note taking needs to improve. She comes to class unprepared. She does not have a good system for recording her notes. And she has no strategy for reviewing her notes. Like Keena, you too may face some challenges when you take notes. Does any of this sound familiar? Let's see how we can improve your note taking.

Many students resist this topic because it asks them to examine and change some very deeply rooted habits. What you have done in the past may be working, but it can be improved. If some of your

How can I be more intentional about note taking?

What system of note taking will work best for me?

When and how should I review my notes?

habits resemble Keena's, we know that the information offered in this chapter will improve your note-taking skills considerably. In this chapter, you will see the importance of taking notes with intention, of using more than one system, and of reviewing your notes on a regular basis.

Why Take Notes?

Think about it from the standpoint of your instructors for a moment. Your instructors have to choose what information they present to their classes. Do you think they pick information they see as unimportant? Of course they do not. They pick out information that they see as *most* important. That information will likely show up on their exams.

So is taking notes really that important? Yes. Notes are the key to remembering important information shared during class time. In fact, if you don't take any notes, you may be unable to recall even the basic points of a lecture. Consider your notes to be tools that will help you succeed in school. Finally, even if you don't verbally participate in class, you are actively participating by taking notes. Students who take notes are more engaged with the subject matter. By engaging the subject matter, you have already started the learning process.

Be Intentional

What does it mean to "be intentional" when you take notes? It means that you attend class, prepare for class, and maintain your attention during class.

Attendance

First, you must attend all your classes. This is essential to your success. Your presence in class shows your instructor that you are serious about the class. Furthermore, your presence allows you to take notes. Some students skip class and get the notes from someone else. By doing this, they have missed a key step in the learning process. You can compare your notes with another student's, but this should only be done to fill in areas you may have missed.

Preparation

Being intentional about note taking also means coming to class prepared. Besides having important materials like a notebook and a pen,

PhotoDisc/gettyimages, 2002

this also means mentally preparing yourself to listen. Spend the minutes before class reviewing previous notes and any reading assignments. This refreshes your memory for the subject matter and helps you become mentally ready to proceed with class. Always date your notes, and write on one side of the paper so your notes remain easy to read.

Attentiveness

The third part of being intentional means that you are attentive throughout the class. Ideally, when you take notes, you are actively *listening* rather than simply *hearing*. There is a difference between listening and hearing. You can hear sounds like a clock ticking, cars rushing past an open window, or someone shouting your name across a crowded room. But active listening requires that you concentrate and cognitively process what is being said.

Do you have trouble paying attention? Try the following techniques:

Say to yourself, "I'm going to actively listen now" when the instructor starts.

Focus on the instructor—not on distractions.

Think about the subject matter and try to anticipate the next points.

Box 8.1

Defeat Your Distractions

Not paying attention during class is a habit. You can blame the instructor, the class subject, or the person across the aisle, but in reality, your level of attention is your habit. If you are in the habit of becoming inattentive during class, try the following exercise. Put a blank sheet of paper next to your notes on the desk. Put a small mark on the page every time you catch your mind wandering from the lecture. At first, you may have a lot of marks on the page. But you will find that the number of marks will decrease if you continue the exercise. By thinking more actively about where your attention lies during class, you will begin the process of defeating distractions.

Avoid becoming mentally distracted if you disagree with something. Listen to the entire message before you respond.

If the subject matter is difficult or you feel your attention starting to slip, remind yourself that this class is important to your success. Briefly recall the goals you set for this class and push yourself to listen.

Watch for changes in the instructor's enthusiasm, intensity, and the use of visual aids to determine what information the instructor thinks is important.

Proceed with a System

Not every class is the same. So it is important for you to have more than one note-taking system. This means evaluating the class subject matter, the nature of the class, and the lecture style of the instructor before deciding on a style of note taking. You may already be familiar with some of the systems that follow, but be open to the possibility that your current system may not work as well as the ones presented here. One system of note taking may work well in one class but not in another. Remember, be intentional about your note-taking habits and decide which style is best for each class.

Outlines

Outlines work well with instructors whose lectures are organized into major and minor ideas that flow in an orderly way. If your instructor offers a main idea and then expands on the idea with more detailed minor points, try outlining as your system for taking notes.

Topic: Narrative Criticism
Date: September 20, 2002

I. What Is Narrative Criticism?

Narrative criticism is the careful analysis of the author's artful selection of content and form when telling a story.

II. What Components of a Story Need to Be Analyzed?
   A. The Plot
      The plot is the organizing principle of the story. It has a beginning, middle, and ending.
   B. The Characterization
      Authors invite us to meet characters in a variety of ways.
      1. The character speaks.
      2. The character is spoken about.
      3. The character acts.
      4. The character's appearance is described.
      5. The character is named.
   C. The Shaping of Time
      1. Duration
      2. Sequence

Paragraphs

Not all lectures can be recorded using an outline. Some instructors seem to jump from one idea to another. If the lecturer takes leaps from one point to another that are hard to follow and then backtracks to what was said earlier, try using paragraph style. These notes don't have to be grammatically complete sentences. However, they should capture the main elements of the idea being presented. Leave lots of space within your notes if you choose this style. Later, when you review your notes, you can add extra information or rewrite sections to make your notes clearer.

Topic: Narrative Criticism
Date: September 20, 2002

What Is Narrative Criticism?

Narr. crit. =
careful analysis of the author's artful selection of content and form when telling story.

What Components of a Story Need to Be Analyzed?

The plot is the org. prin. of the story . . . a beginning, middle, and ending.

The Characterization
How? Watch for the character speaking, spoken about, acting, appearance, and naming.

The Shaping of Time
How? Duration and sequence of time.

Recall Columns

This system is based on the Cornell format developed by Walter Pauk. (For more information on this system, see Walter Pauk, *How to Study in College,* 6th edition, New York: Houghton Mifflin, 1997.) For each page of your notes, draw a vertical line the length of the page 3 inches from the left. This will create two columns. During class, take notes only on the right side of the page. This is called the record column. After class, when you are reviewing your notes, fill in key words and questions in the left column. This is the recall column.

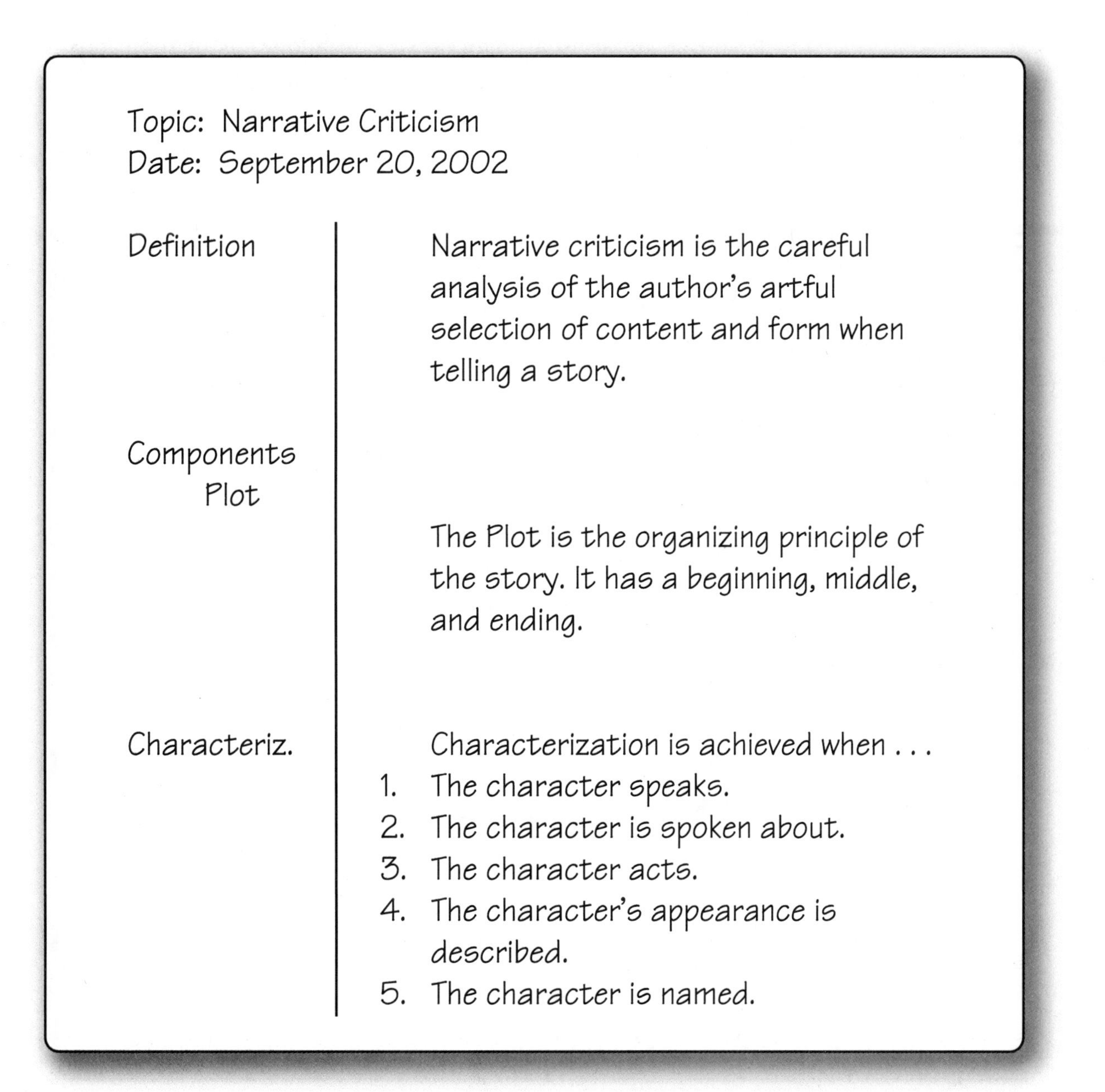

Visual Maps

Sometimes the information presented in class may be easier to remember if you create a visual map. This technique might be difficult to do as the instructor speaks, so you might have to create your visual map during your review session later that same day. But the effort is worth it, especially if you are a visual or kinesthetic learner. Creating a visual map gives your brain a chance to "picture" the information. This may make it easier for you to recall the information in the future. Visual maps easily illustrate relationships between concepts. You may recall the relationships more easily in a visual map than in outline or paragraph form.

If you create a visual map, be sure to allow lots of room on the paper. The center of the paper contains the main concept, and related points radiate from the center. You can even use different colors to identify the main points.

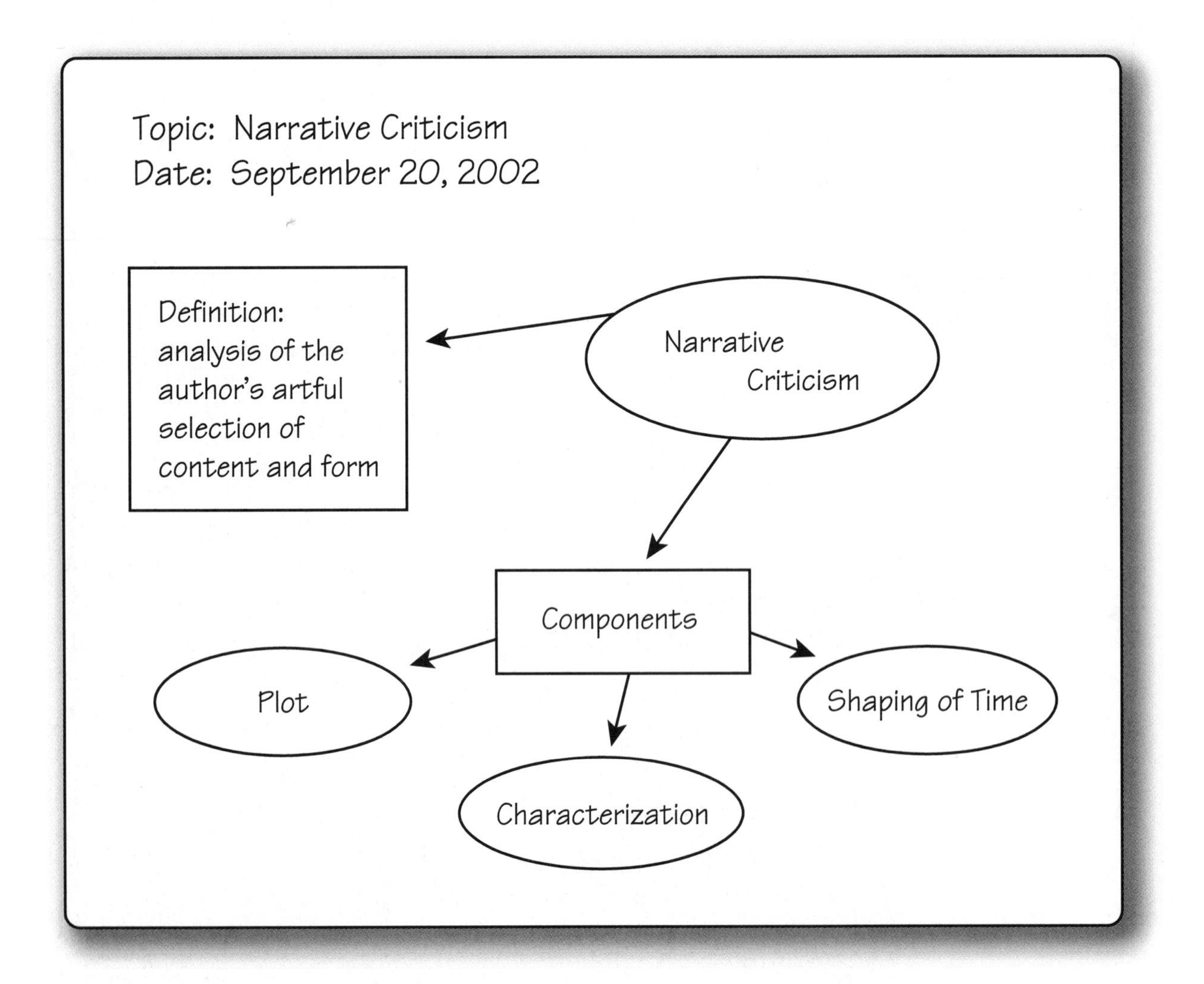

General Tips for Any Note-Taking System

Even after you have chosen a method for taking notes, there are some basic tips that will help you be a more effective note taker regardless of the system you use.

Leave blank spaces. Always be generous with the blank space you leave in your notes. This leaves room for information you can add during your review.

Record information from boards, overheads, and computer-generated images. The creation of visual aids takes time. The instructor considers this information important.

Ask if you don't understand something. Don't be afraid to raise your hand and ask the instructor to repeat or explain difficult material. If you are not comfortable asking during class, stay after class for a few minutes and speak to the instructor one on one.

Use a "lost" signal. If you get lost in class and are unable to complete a section of your notes, mark your notes so that you know where they are going to be incomplete. The "lost" signal will remind you to recover what you missed either from the instructor or a classmate.

Record main ideas, not each word. Your goal in note taking should not be a word-for-word transcription of the lecture. Instead, your goal is to record the main points of the class.

Box 8.2

Get a Partner

Consider asking another student in class to be your note-taking partner. This might sound unusual, but here are some benefits.

- This is a safety net to ensure you don't miss important information.
- Knowing that you will be comparing your notes might motivate you to listen more closely in class. As a result, you will take more complete notes.
- You also might take neater notes knowing another student will be looking at them.
- If you miss class due to an emergency, you can get a copy of your partner's notes.
- Create weekly review sessions with your partner. This will be invaluable study time for both of you.
- Exchange phone numbers or e-mail addresses so you can contact each other with questions.
- Remember, this is a partnership. Don't rely on your partner to take notes for you.

End with Review

Your class might be over, but you still have one more step to complete in the note-taking process. It is vital to review your notes. Let's consider when and how you might review your notes.

When?

Since much of the lecture will be forgotten by the next day, plan to review your notes within 24 hours of taking them. Designate review sessions into your time-management plan if you have not done so already. This doesn't need to be a big block of time. Find three 10-minute blocks during the day or maybe 30 minutes in the evening.

How?

You have produced a valuable study tool. Now it is time to use it. Don't just silently reread your notes. Make this an active learning time.

- Enter key words in the recall column.
- Create a visual map to supplement your existing notes.
- Fill in blank spaces with notes from the readings and enhance your notes from your own memory.
- Recite your notes out loud. After you recite them, try to describe the concepts in your own words without looking at your notes.

Whatever you choose to do, make it an active learning time. Remember this important step. The time you spend reviewing your notes now is time invested in study for your future exams.

Like Keena, there is room for you to improve your note-taking system. Be intentional when you take notes, choose a system for note taking that fits each class, and schedule time to review your notes. It may be a challenge for you to change your habits, but you are responsible for your climb up the pyramid of success. Effective note taking is a vital component of that climb. Don't give up! You are on the edge of successful note taking.

CRITICAL REFLECTION EXERCISE

Fit the System to Your Class

In the beginning of this chapter, we said note taking needs to be an intentional activity. Now it is time for you to be intentional. Think about each class you have and determine which method is most appropriate.

Class: ______________________________

The best system for taking notes in this class is:

____

____

The best time to review my notes for this class is:

____

____

I will review my notes using these methods:

____

____

Class: ______________________________

The best system for taking notes in this class is:

____

____

The best time to review my notes for this class is:

____

____

I will review my notes using these methods:

____

____

Class: ______________________________

The best system for taking notes in this class is:

____

____

The best time to review my notes for this class is:

____

____

I will review my notes using these methods:

____

____

Class: ______________________________

The best system for taking notes in this class is:

____

____

The best time to review my notes for this class is:

____

____

I will review my notes using these methods:

____

____

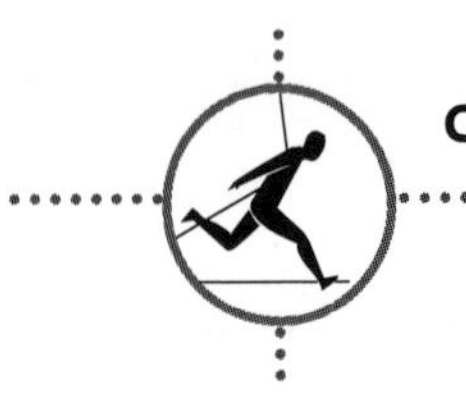

CRITICAL THINKING EXERCISE

Note-Taking Experiment

After completing the preceding exercise, pick one class and try the new approach you have described. Spend 2 weeks using the new techniques for note taking and reviewing. Then evaluate how successful your approach is and make adjustments as needed. ●

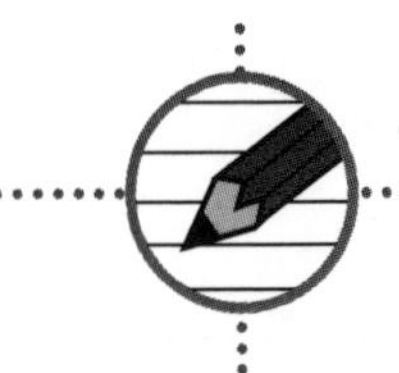

JOURNAL

Pick one of your classes that requires a lot of note taking. Ask three of your classmates for photocopies of their notes from one of the class sessions. Look at the content. In your journal, answer the following questions. How was the information you recorded the same or different from theirs? Compare their note-taking system to your own. How is it similar? How is it different? In which ways were their note-taking systems weaker or stronger than your own? ●

ON THE NET

For more advice and direction on improving your note taking, go to Wadsworth's Your College Success Resource Center. Go to www.success.wadsworth.com. Click on "Discipline Resources" and then on "Resource Web Links." Under the "Resource Web Links," click on "Study Skills" and surf those links for more tips. You will find interesting information about listening at www.listen.org/pages/factoids.html. You can also find additional resources and exercises for *On the Edge of Success* at http://info.wadsworth.com/clason. ●

9

Score on Your Exams

This topic is not new to you. As long as you have been in school, you have been taking tests. College is no different. Exams play a major role in the grade you receive in most college courses. So if you are getting low grades in the your college courses, you are most likely getting low scores on exams. If you want to improve your grade point average (GPA), finding strategies to improve your exam scores is essential. No one is more aware of this than the college student on academic probation. That makes this topic critical for you as you climb the pyramid of success.

You already know some things about college exams. First of all, you are tested less frequently than you were in high school. Therefore, every college exam is worth more in the course's grading system. It also means you are tested on considerably more material than you were in the typical high school class. You may have been able to study for a high school test in 1 or 2 hours. But since the typical college exam has 10 to 20 times more material to review, you need to spend at least 7 to 10 hours studying for such an exam.

So what can you do differently? The answer may not be to spend more time. You may already have spent 10 hours studying for an exam, reading and rereading the notes, only to be disappointed in the results. Successful exam preparation is not necessarily about spending long hours reading your

How can I improve my preparation time?

How can I improve my memory?

What strategies can I use when taking an exam?

How can I manage my anxiety?

notes time after time. Successful exam preparation is about planning more widely spaced study sessions in which you creatively review and recite the material. In this chapter, we offer you tips on preparing for your exams, taking your exams, and managing the anxiety that is a part of that process. We believe that if you put these tips into practice, you will improve your exam grades and your GPA.

Memorization and Preparation Plan

When you prepare for an exam, you are attempting to put information into your long-term memory so that you can retrieve it at the time of the exam. It is rather easy to put things into your short-term memory. But typically, that memory bank is limited to five to nine items that can be held for a period of 20–30 seconds. That is great for ordering at a restaurant but not much help for the history exam. You need to recall that material for more than 20–30 seconds.

So how can you put your history notes into long-term memory? This kind of memorization involves three steps: encoding, storing, and retrieving. During the encoding step, you come into contact with information and translate it into something you can understand. The second step involves storing the information in long-term memory. During this step, you select the details that you want to remember, organize those details, and plant them in your memory. During your homework time, you will spend more time in this step than you will in the other two. The final step is retrieving the information from long-term storage so you can use it when you take an exam.

If you are going to plant items in your long-term memory, you need to creatively review the material again and again over an extended period of time. The following information is designed to help you develop and refine your exam preparation plan.

Scope

Begin your preparation by determining the scope of the exam. What is going to be on the test? You cannot remember everything, so you need to be selective in what you study. This allows you to focus on the content that is most critical to your success. Find out all you can about the exam. Will it be on the course lectures, class discussions, textbook, handouts, or out-of-class assignments? Will the exam cover material from the entire semester to date or just the last unit studied? Check the syllabus, listen for your instructor's comments about the exam, and

PhotoDisc/gettyimages, 2002

don't hesitate to ask the instructor for clarification if you are not sure. The more you can limit the scope of your study, the more you will be able to master that content.

Type of Exam

It is also helpful to know the type of exam you will be taking. Objective tests that contain true-false, matching, and multiple-choice questions focus more on facts. Essay tests ask you to have a background in the facts but expect you to manipulate ideas creatively. Your study strategy will be different for each. We will talk more specifically about the types of exams later, but be sure to find out what kind of exam your instructor is most likely to give.

Schedule

Students who are less successful with exams often do all their exam preparation the night before the exam is given. Since there is a limit to how much information you can digest at one sitting, this approach prevents students from getting the information into long-term memory. So when you think about your exam preparation schedule, think about extending that preparation time over several days. We are not necessarily talking about more preparation time, but the spacing of that preparation time over the week before the exam. This means making up a schedule that allows you to study the information you want to remember in shorter and more widely spaced sessions.

This kind of daily review strengthens the path to long-term storage. First, determine the total amount of time you need to prepare. At a minimum, we suggest you consider 7 to 10 hours for a typical college exam. If that seems like a lot of time, remember how critical these exams are to your course grade. Design your study schedule so that you spend 1 hour studying each day for 7 to 10 days before the exam. Then add a second 1-hour session the day before the exam just to pull everything together.

Review and Recitation

How are you going to use those 10 hours of study time? Won't rereading your notes get boring? Yes, it would! So don't plan on just reading your notes over and over again. Your goal is to review and recite the information in as many different ways as possible. This keeps the process from getting old and helps you remember the material you are studying.

You can review the information by rereading it, by reorganizing facts as you rewrite them on visual maps, by condensing the material on note cards, and by combining information on charts. You can recite the material aloud by going to a study group or by teaching someone else. Check the following list for ways that you can review and recite your exam material.

- Create a summary sheet that lists the key terms and concepts from your notes. This condenses all you need to know on one sheet of paper.
- Make flashcards to help you recall key dates, terms, textbook questions, or formulas.
- Recite from the exam review sheet supplied by your instructor or your summary sheet.
- Have a friend quiz you using the exam review sheet supplied by your instructor or your summary sheet.
- Create visual maps on all or a portion of the exam material.
- Practice mathematical problems from examples in your textbook.
- Practice answering essay questions you create.
- Start a study group and discuss the material with others.
- Go to a supplemental instruction session.

- Recite the answers to textbook questions out loud.
- Teach someone else the material on which you will be tested.
- Answer the questions at the end of your textbook's chapters that are included on the test.
- Create memory aids for more difficult material.
- Get tutoring sponsored by your college.

The Day Before

If you have studied for the exam over the past week, the day before the test will become the final review. The class session before the exam is an important part of your final preparation. Some students skip this class to work on their own, but that may mean they miss something very important. During the class before the exam, professors often conduct a review session or give key information about the exam itself.

We also suggest that the day before the exam should look very much like the other days of your week. Many students change their diet, sleep, and study patterns. We suggest you avoid any dramatic changes. Keep your sleep pattern intact. You want to be well rested and alert when you write. Besides, if you conduct a final review before you sleep, your sleep will actually help cement those memories in place because you will be eliminating new competing data. Be sure that you eat well and avoid caffeine and sugar loading. Changes in your caffeine or sugar intake will lead to highs and lows that disrupt the process of memory and impair effective exam performance.

Test-Taking Plan

Now that you have prepared yourself to take the exam, let's talk about some tips you may use during the actual writing of the exam. These techniques are not a substitute for the preparation strategy we have discussed, but they will help you manage the time and content of the exam so that you may write more successfully.

Overview

After you have placed your name on the exam, be sure to spend 4 or 5 minutes looking over its contents and planning a writing strategy. Which portions of the exam will be easier for you and which will be more difficult? What point value is assigned to various parts of the exam? Don't be fooled. Several pages of multiple-choice questions may have the same value as one essay question!

Once you have determined the difficulty of the questions and their point values, plan your time. Figure out how many minutes to allow for each section. Write that value in the margin so that you don't invest too much time in one area at the expense of another. As you set up the time schedule, be sure to allow time at the end of the exam period to go over the test and review your answers. Revisit those difficult questions and check answers that are obviously wrong or questions you neglected to answer. Undoubtedly, other students will leave the room before you. That is okay. Your goal is not to finish early but to demonstrate your knowledge of the material and get the best grade you can.

Do the Easy Questions First

No matter how much you have prepared for the exam, you need to boost your confidence early in the process. Don't just start with the first question on the first page. Start with the questions you know best. This warms up your thinking engine as well as builds your self-confidence for the more challenging portions of the exam.

Objective Test Questions

Multiple-choice exams, true-false exams, and matching exams primarily measure your ability to deal with facts. When you are taking a multiple-choice exam, be sure to read the stem of the question carefully and think of the answer before looking at the options you are given. Those options contain "distracting" statements that are designed to look inviting although they are wrong. Envision what the right answer should look like and then eliminate inaccurate or less complete answers.

Watch out for words like *always, all, never,* and *only.* These choices are usually incorrect. Also be aware of choices that contain the words *not, except,* and *but.* These short words completely change the meaning of the answer.

Some of the same things apply to writing true-false tests. Read the statement very carefully. Everything in the sentence must be true if you are going to mark it as a true statement. Some words in the statement may be so powerful that they allow for no exceptions. A sentence with *always, never,* and *only* is usually false. *Often* and *frequently* may be found in statements that are true. Be sure to read through the entire exam to see if information in one question will help you answer another question about which you are unsure.

The matching section of an exam usually consists of two columns that need to be connected to one another. One column contains the term and the other its definition or description. Read both columns before you begin to answer. Match the terms about which you are sure first. This will narrow your options when you need to begin making more "educated guesses."

Essay Questions

Essay exams are the most challenging of the exams you will write. They measure not only your knowledge of the facts but your ability to think effectively with those facts. As you confront an essay question, be sure that you read the question carefully. Students often fail to write an effective essay because they are not responding to the question being asked.

Look for and mark three elements within the essay question that will drive your answer in the right direction. Every essay question will ask you to respond to a *topic* or *topics*. It will contain a *key word* that asks you to do something specific with that topic (describe, analyze, prove, etc.). There will also be a *limiting word* or *phrase* that focuses the answer to a specific scenario. Here is an example of an essay question:

Describe the way in which Bernoulli's principle of pressure makes it possible for an airplane to fly.

Even though you may not know the answer to the question, you can pick out these three components. The topic of this essay question is "Bernoulli's principle of pressure," the key word is "describe," and the limiting phrase is "airplane to fly." These three items should be present in the first sentence of your essay. We call that your topic sentence. By writing a topic sentence in this way, you begin your response in a way that is focused and on target. The answer to this essay question might begin like this:

Bernoulli's principle of pressure makes it possible for an airplane to fly by . . .

It is a good idea to write the outline of the response in the margin. This gives you a plan to follow as you write your answer. It also keeps the answer moving in a logical direction that is on target. If the answer has more than one part, be certain that you clearly identify those parts with paragraph breaks or obvious language clues like "first" and "second." Instructors may lower the grade of answers that ramble aimlessly. Keep your answer to the point, neat, and grammatically correct. See Box 9.1 on the following page for the most common key words used in essay tests.

Box 9.1

Key Words in Essay Questions

Here are the tasks that instructors may ask you to perform in the key word dimension of an essay question.

Analyze—to break the topic or problem into its parts to understand it. Discuss and examine each part and show how the parts work together within the larger framework of the topic.

Compare—to examine the characteristics or qualities of several topics and identify their similarities.

Contrast—to examine the characteristics or qualities of several topics and identify their differences. Compare and contrast are often combined in one question.

Critique—to evaluate the quality of a statement or idea. A critique acknowledges positive and negative qualities. You may need to supplement your opinions with support from recognized expert testimony.

Define—to give the accurate and concise meaning of a word or phrase. Providing an example may help clarify a definition, but an example is not itself a definition.

Describe—to give a verbal account of something. This can be in a narrative or other form of description that lists characteristics or qualities.

Discuss—to examine important characteristics of a topic or issue. Discussion often includes identifying the main points and the important questions within the topic.

Evaluate—to weigh the strengths, weakness, merits, worth, or truthfulness of a topic or argument.

Explain—to make a concept or topic understandable. Explanations often treat how and why things develop.

Illustrate—to give concrete examples of something. This may be either in written form or in a diagram or picture.

Interpret—to explain the meaning or meaningfulness of something.

Justify—to argue in support of a position by giving evidence or reasons in its favor. Provide logical reasoning and concrete examples to support your argument.

Narrate—to tell a story or describe a series of events in chronological order.

Box 9.1 (continued)

Outline—to give the main points of a topic in appropriate order, focusing on broader concepts.

Prove—to demonstrate the truth of a statement by providing facts or logical arguments.

Relate—to identify the connections or relationships between topics or events.

Review—to summarize the main parts of a topic. Evaluation may also be included.

Summarize—to briefly cover the main points of a topic, omitting details. A summary covers all the most important points, yet remains a condensed account of the topic.

Trace—to describe the order of events or the development of an idea.

Anxiety

Everyone feels some degree of anxiety when taking an exam. It is our body's natural reaction to a perceived threat. You may experience butterflies, loss of sleep, irritability, nausea, loss of appetite, diarrhea, headaches, or loss of concentration. If you are bothered by these symptoms, here are some things you can do to diminish this anxiety.

First of all, don't give an exam more power than it is due. An exam is a tool designed to measure your knowledge of a body of information on a certain day. Its power is very, very limited. It does not measure your general intelligence, character, creativity, or value as a person. So don't agonize over the anticipated outcome of an exam.

Preparation is also an important factor in reducing your anxiety. Follow the plan outlined earlier in the chapter and you will also be working to reduce your exam anxiety. We tend to fear the unknown, so learn all you can about the scope and nature of the exam. Review and recite the material according to our plan and you will diminish your anxiety.

Don't allow anxiety to wash over you because you don't know the answer to a question. Admit from the start that you will not know everything for the exam. Despite your best efforts, there will be a question for which you have not prepared. There will be questions that you get wrong. Accept that fact and move on. You don't have to be perfect to pass a test.

Box 9.2 *Memory Aids*

Poems and acrostics may help you recall concepts or lists of facts. When you needed to figure out how many days there are in the month of April, you may have relied on the poem, "Thirty days hath September, April, June, and November. All the rest have thirty-one." Here is a poem to help you recall the resignation of President Nixon in 1974. "In 1974, Richard Nixon hit the floor."

An acrostic can help you recall lists of things. AROW helps pilots remember which documents they need to have in their airplane to fly it legally. AROW stands for airworthiness certificate, registration, operating limitations, and weight and balance information. You may have difficulty recalling the different forms of chemical bonds if you had to recall the list of ionic bonds, covalent bonds, and polar bonds. Forming the acrostic "PIC bonds" can help you remember that information.

There are also certain kinds of people you want to avoid in the days before the exam. You know the kind of people we mean. They are the panic-stricken people who wander the lounges and halls of your school talking about how terrible the coming exam is going to be and how everyone will do poorly on it. If you find yourself negatively influenced by these preachers of doom and gloom, stay away from them.

Finally, use relaxation strategies both before and after the exam. When you notice that you are tightening your muscles and breathing more quickly than is necessary, make a conscious effort to relax your muscles and slow your breathing. For some, anxiety can be so significant that these strategies are not enough. If you cannot overcome your anxiety on your own, talk to a professional counselor on your campus for more suggestions on how to diminish exam anxiety.

Exams will play a major role in your course grades. We have spoken about ways to effectively prepare for an exam, ways to effectively take an exam, and methods to diminish your anxiety. Put these strategies to work in your life and you will be on the edge of successful exam performance.

CRITICAL REFLECTION EXERCISE

Find Your Challenges

All of us find some types of exams more challenging than others. Let's find out where you are vulnerable. Examine four or five tests that you have taken in the past. Determine where you are losing the most points.

Type of Questions	Test 1	Test 2	Test 3	Test 4	Test 5
Multiple-Choice					
True-False					
Matching					
Essay					

Do some more reading online about the kind of exam question that gives you the most trouble. If you find that you are making mistakes equally among all types of questions, check the quality of your study techniques. ●

EXERCISE

Build a Time Plan

Now it is time for you to experiment with a time plan. Pick an exam that is coming in the next couple of weeks and make an exam plan with which you will experiment. Complete the following plan and put it to work. Be sure to divide up the content of the exam and determine which review or recitation technique you will use each day of the review. ●

Exam Plan

Course: ____________________

Date of Exam: ____________________

Scope of Exam: ____________________

____

Type of Exam: ____________________

____

Study Schedule:

Day	Time	Content	Review and Recitation Technique
10			
9			
8			
7			
6			
5			
4			
3			
2			
1			

JOURNAL

Let's see what you can learn from other successful students. Visit with five upperclass students who have found ways to be successful in their classwork. Ask them the following questions:

What do you do to take exams more effectively?

What do you do to reduce anxiety when you take exams?

In your journal, write about what you discovered and reflect on how you will use what you have discovered. ●

ON THE NET

For more advice and direction on improving your exam performance, go to Wadsworth's Your College Success Resource Center. Go to www.success.wadsworth.com. Click on "Discipline Resources" and then on "Resource Web Links." Under the "Resource Web Links," click on "Study Skills" and surf those links. You may also click on "Study Skills/Strategies" under "Discipline Resources" for more tips. For more information on stress and anxiety management, see www.unc.edu/depts/unc_caps/resources.htm. You can also find additional resources and exercises for *On the Edge of Success* at http://info.wadsworth.com/clason. ●

10

Write to Make an Impression

Have you ever stared at a blank sheet of paper or a blinking cursor on a computer screen wishing that the words to a "perfect" introduction would flow from your fingers? Let's face it, excellent papers rarely happen on the first try. Yet some students put off their writing assignments until a few days or hours before it is due. Because the pressure is on, the first draft has to be the last. If that sounds like you, then you know writing a paper can be an excruciating, pressure-filled task. It can be a burden rather than an opportunity to share your thinking with others. Good writing takes preparation, research, organization, revision, and lots of planning.

College trains you to be a better thinker. Writing helps in that process by placing the way you think before your eyes. You can see the strengths and the weaknesses of your thinking when it is on paper. Writing not only improves your ability to think, but it is also one way to share your thinking with others. Writing, like speaking, is a means of expressing your thoughts and ideas. Becoming a capable student means you can effectively communicate through writing. In this chapter, we present each step of the writing process from understanding the purpose of the assignment to revising your final draft.

How can I plan my writing projects?

What should I do before I start writing?

How can I improve the quality of my writing?

Understand the Assignment

This first step might surprise you. Before you begin a paper, it is essential that you fully understand the *purpose* of the assignment. This means more than knowing the mechanics such as the number of pages or that it must be type-written. You need to understand the purpose to know the goal of the assignment. Is the paper an informative research review? Is it a persuasive position paper? If you are not sure about the purpose of the paper, ask the instructor. Here are some common types of papers.

Position Paper

Sometimes called an essay, this type of paper requires you to discuss your views on a certain topic. For example, your political science teacher might ask you to write an essay about your position on a recent election issue.

Critical Reaction Paper

After discussing a topic in class or reading an article, your instructor may ask you to write a reaction paper. Write about where you agreed, where you disagreed, and why. Study the evidence. Does it clearly support the conclusions? Is the evidence outdated? Try to understand and dissect the logic behind any arguments presented in the literature. You may have several reactions to the topic, so be sure to organize your reactions clearly in the paper.

Case Study

Perhaps your instructor wants you to conduct an in-depth review of a person or an event. This is a case study. Although the parameters of this type of paper vary, be sure to provide ample details and anecdotes.

Research Paper

This type is probably the most time-consuming project because of the amount of library research it entails. You need to gather information and organize it into a well-crafted presentation. Because of the complexity of this project and the amount of time it consumes, the research paper usually counts more heavily toward your final course grade. An early start on this type of paper is essential.

Create a Writing Plan

It is important to create a time-management plan for each paper, particularly the longer research paper assignments. You need to set your own "due dates" for each step in the writing process. If the assignment requires outside research, plan for that too. Create a plan similar to this:

September 25: Pick a topic and check it out with the instructor.

October 15: Complete the initial research for the topic.

October 20: Create a thesis statement and working outline.

October 27: Complete additional research.

November 10: Complete the first draft.

November 15: Revise the first draft.

November 22: Go to the writing center on campus for feedback on your paper.

November 30: Complete the final draft.

December 3: Paper due in class.

December 4: Celebrate! Reward yourself with a hot fudge sundae and movie.

Even if the assignment doesn't entail research, still set due dates for a thesis statement, working outline, first draft, revisions, and completed project. When you break down your larger paper assignments into manageable steps, you will be able to stay on top of the assignment. This is the way you create a writing plan.

Get Ready to Write

There are lots of steps to complete before you actually start to write your first draft, but sometimes students shortcut these steps because they run out of time. Plan carefully and take advantage of the prewriting strategies offered in this section. Remember to answer two important questions. What do I want to say? How do I want to say it?

What Do I Want to Say?

Writing a paper is a chance to expand and refine your knowledge of a topic. It can be a chance for you to persuade an audience about a topic that is especially important to you. Keep these benefits in mind when you write your papers. Don't think of them as burdens, but as opportunities and chances for you to take the lead in learning about a new issue or event. If you struggle with writing papers, work through the following steps before you start to write. You might be surprised that writing the first draft will be easier than it had been in the past.

Picking a Topic Sometimes your instructor will assign a specific topic for your paper. Other times, you will have the freedom to select your own topic. This freedom can present a problem for some students. Because there is so much information available, the choices are overwhelming. Do not let this become the reason you put off writing your paper.

The only way to find a topic is to look for one. If no topic springs to mind, go to the library and start skimming newspapers, magazines, indexes, or journals. As you skim these sources, be aware of times you stop skimming and start reading an article with interest. Keep a list of the topics that you read. After an hour of skimming, look at your list of topics. Chances are something on that list will spark your interest. The more interested you are in a topic, the more motivated you will be to complete it.

Brainstorming After you have chosen your topic, spend some time thinking about it. What do you already know about the topic? What do you want to discover about the topic? This can actually help you narrow the topic into a manageable paper. Let's say that you want to write a paper on the death penalty. That is an enormous topic. Brainstorm with a friend or two. Write the topic in the center of a piece of paper and talk about all the dimensions and issues related to the death penalty. Your notes might look like this.

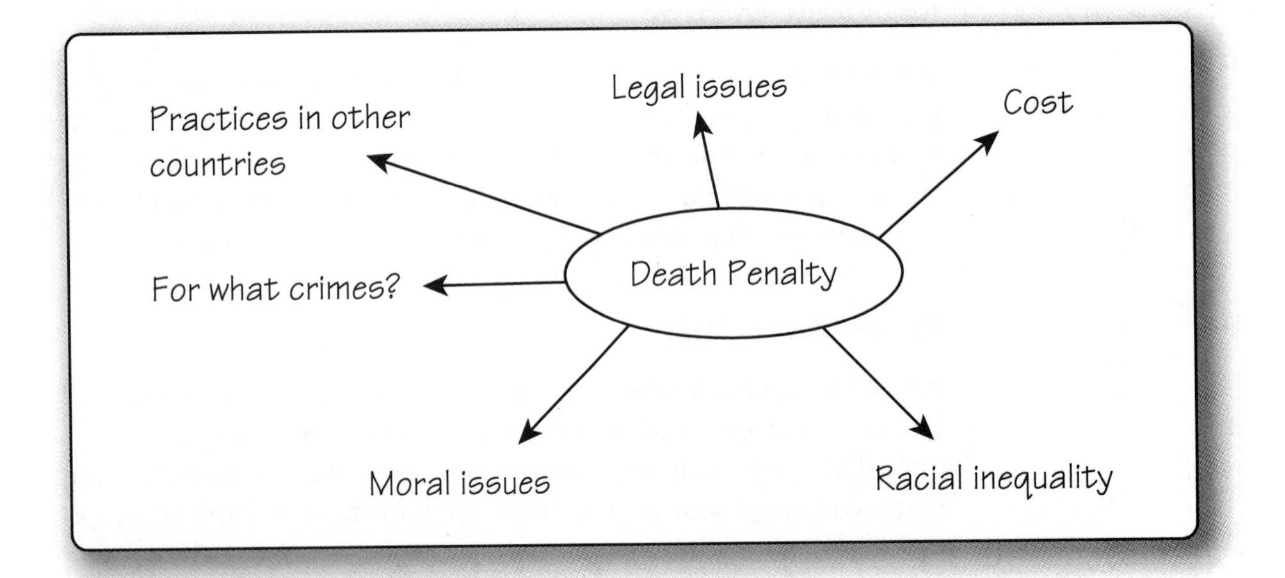

PhotoDisc/gettyimages, 2002

Freewriting You can also use freewriting as a way to generate the direction of your topic. Just start writing whatever comes to your mind when you think about the topic. Don't worry about spelling, grammar, punctuation, or organization. Just keep your fingers moving! Set a timer and freewrite for 10 minutes. Explore various dimensions of the topic. When you are finished, look over what you have written and highlight the ideas that are of most interest to you.

Initial Research As we have said, some assignments, such as reaction papers, don't involve much, if any, research. But other types of assignments ask you to engage with the thinking of others by doing research. Once you have a clear understanding of your topic, go to the library and start your research. Your goal for this stage of the research is to get a general overview of the issue. What are the main points? What are the basic arguments? What issues are being debated? Learn enough to create a thesis statement and working outline.

Thesis Statement What do you want to say? Write out a sentence that captures the essence of what you want your paper to present. For example, let's say you are to write a research paper on the United States during World War II. After brainstorming, you decide you want to focus on the role of women during the war effort. After doing your initial research, your thesis statement might look like this: "The development of the Women's Airforce Service Pilots (WASP) was critical to the success of the United States' Air Force during World War II."

How Do I Want to Say It?

Now that you have written your thesis statement, it is time to organize the information into a logical, cohesive order.

Working Outline Creating an outline will help you organize all the information you have gathered so far. Start with the main points you wish to cover in your paper. What do you want your reader to know? What evidence will you use to persuade your reader? Then add the subpoints that will further explain and support your main ideas. This is a working outline, so some of the components might be shifted as you write. You may also decide to add points or delete existing points as you write.

Additional Research Once you create an outline, you may discover that you need to strengthen your own understanding further with a return to the library. Your outline will help you pinpoint exactly where your paper needs more information and evidence. Once this step is complete, you are ready to write.

Write the First Draft

When you follow the ideas and steps just presented, writing the first draft won't seem like such a daunting task. You have done a great deal of work already. Simply follow your outline and refer to your research notes as you write each section. Above all, write this first draft *knowing you will revise the paper later.* There is no pressure on you to write perfect paragraphs. Here are some tips you may use in writing the first draft.

- Don't criticize your work or linger over one sentence with which you are struggling. Save the critical analysis for later.
- Although the introduction contains the first words your reader will read, it may not be the first words you write. If you don't have a clear introduction in mind, let it go. As you write the paper, ideas for the introduction will occur to you.
- If you have information from outside sources, cite these sources in your paper. Any words or ideas that are not your own need to be credited to the original author. Be sure to find out what preference

Box 10.1 ***The Perils of Plagiarism***

Plagiarism is using someone else's words or ideas as your own. The outside research from which you draw your information is considered the "intellectual property" of the author. When you use that intellectual property in your paper, you must give the appropriate credit to that author. Do not pass off someone else's work as your own. In addition, just changing a few words from another author's paragraph is still considered plagiarism. If you quote directly from a source or express the ideas of a source in your own words, you must give credit to the author. Most instructors and colleges have very stiff penalties for plagiarism. Don't risk it.

your instructor has when it comes to referencing outside sources in the paper (e.g., American Psychological Association, Modern Language Association, Turabian). Check your library, learning center, or bookstore for the most recent edition of the style you will use.

- Don't let your conclusion fizzle. This is a crucial part of the paper. Give yourself time to really work on this section. This is the last section your instructor reads before assigning a grade, so end the paper with a strong conclusion.

After your first draft is complete, it is a good idea to take a short break from the material. Put it away for a day or two. When you return to the paper to revise it, you will be able to look at it with a fresh perspective.

Revise the Draft

Now it is time to revise your work. The more time you spend revising your papers, the better writer you will become. Use the following suggestions to revise your initial draft.

Be a Critical Reader

As you wrote your first draft, you were concerned with getting all the necessary information on paper. Now it is time to put yourself in the shoes of your reader by critically reviewing your paper. Do the sections flow logically, or do you need to rearrange the material? Do you have transitions between the main points of the paper so the reader can easily comprehend the organization? Can you rewrite sentences using the active voice rather than passive voice? Do the quotations fit smoothly into the text of the paper? Are your arguments well-supported by your research? Are you using gender-neutral language? Try to read the paper as if you were your instructor assigning a grade to it. What are the strong points? Where are the weak points?

Read It Out Loud

One of the best revising techniques is to read your paper out loud. You will be able to identify awkward phrases and sentences much more easily. You wrote the paper. If you stumble over an odd choice of words, you know for certain that your reader will too.

Check for Grammar and Spelling Errors

Since you want your reader to focus on your ideas, you don't want your reader distracted by spelling and grammar errors. Proofread your paper with a dictionary and grammar rule book within arm's reach. Use the spelling checker on your computer but remember that it will not catch every spelling error. For example, it will not indicate a spelling error in the phrase, "Form 1950 too 1960, the Untied States . . ." If you have a tendency toward these kinds of mistakes, ask a friend to proofread your paper too. But remember, you are ultimately responsible for cleaning up the spelling and grammatical errors of your paper.

Go to the Writing Lab

If your campus has a center where students can get feedback on their papers, take advantage of this opportunity. You will receive some very valuable advice!

Revise Again

Once you have revised the first draft, revise it again in a few days. Your writing will continue to improve through each draft. Revise your drafts according to the following checklist.

- ❑ I have an introduction that catches my reader's attention and previews the main points of my paper.
- ❑ I have logically organized the main points of my paper.
- ❑ I have appropriate transitions between paragraphs.

Box 10.2

So What Did You Get on Your Paper?

Many of your instructors will return papers to you with more than just a grade written on them. They will also write comments about the content and form of the paper. You may be in the habit of ignoring these comments. However, we suggest that you read them and take them very seriously. The comments written on your paper not only tell you why you received the grade but also how you may improve your writing. For example, they may indicate a problem with your organization. They may point to problems with grammar. Or they may indicate a weakness in citing resources. Look for patterns in the comments that you receive on returned papers. They signal ways that you may improve your writing. If the comments are not clear, be sure to ask your instructor to clarify those comments so that you can incorporate them in your next writing assignment.

- ❑ I have supported my arguments with convincing evidence.
- ❑ I have given the appropriate citation to any outside material I have used.
- ❑ I have written a conclusion that summarizes the main points.
- ❑ I have checked for spelling and grammar mistakes.
- ❑ I have taken my paper to the writing center for feedback.

High-quality papers require careful research, writing, and revision. Be sure to understand the assignment and create a writing plan. Know what you want to say and how you want to say it before writing the first draft. When your first draft is complete, revise and revise again. When you do, you will be on the edge of successful writing.

EXERCISE

Create a Writing Plan

Choose a paper assignment you have in another class and apply the techniques we discussed in this chapter. The following worksheet will help you structure your writing plan. ●

The Paper Plan

Class:

Paper:

Final Due Date:

Task	Date for Completion	Done ✔
Know the purpose of the paper		
Select a topic		
Do the initial research		
Create a thesis statement		
Create a working outline		
Complete additional research		
Complete the first draft		
Revise the first draft		
Revise the second draft		
Complete the final draft		

JOURNAL

Take one of your papers to the writing center on your campus or send it to an online writing lab associated with your school. Reflect on your experience. What did you learn about your writing? What are some ways you can improve your writing? ●

ON THE NET

For more advice and direction on improving your writing skills, go to Wadsworth's Your College Success Resource Center at www.success.wadsworth.com. Click on "Discipline Resources" and then on "Resource Web Links." Under the "Resource Web Links," click on

"Reading and Writing" and surf those links for more tips. Your College Success Resource Center also offers a variety of summaries under the heading "Study Skills/Strategies," which is listed under "Discipline Resources." Another useful Internet site is www.andromeda.rutgers.edu/~jlynch/Writing/index.html. This site offers explanations of grammar rules along with advice on writing. Even more online writing assistance is available at www.powa.org. You can also find additional resources and exercises for *On the Edge of Success* at http://info.wadsworth.com/clason. ●

11

Pursue a Healthy Lifestyle

Complete the following quiz.

True/False: The things I eat and drink affect my ability to think.

True/False: Adequate sleep is necessary for me to think at my best.

True/False: High amounts of stress make it difficult for me to concentrate on a task.

College is the place to grow and mature your mind. You read books, you write, and you debate to sharpen your thinking skills. Those thinking skills are generated in the brain, an organ that is housed and fed by your body. Thus, there is a critical link between what you do to your body and how well you are able to think. The statements in the quiz you just took are all true. What you eat and drink, your sleep patterns, and your level of stress all impact your intellectual skills. If you treat your body in a reckless way, you impair your thinking ability. That makes this topic critical to your climb up the pyramid of success. Let's examine your health habits to see how they are contributing to your success and where they may need changing. We will discuss sleep patterns, stress management, and diet.

How much sleep do I really need?

What can I do to diminish my stress?

How can I improve my diet?

Sleep

How Much?

The amount of sleep needed varies from person to person. Roommates may be very similar in many respects, but one roommate may require more sleep than the other. Some people may be able to function with only 4 hours of sleep, but the average individual needs 8 hours to fully rest the body. The amount of sleep needed per night varies between people, but one thing is certain. If you don't get enough sleep, your body will let you know. Insufficient sleep results in poor concentration, feelings of exhaustion, less emotional control, impaired memory, headaches, and decisions of inferior quality. If you are experiencing these symptoms, you may be getting less sleep than you need.

When?

The time of day you sleep can be as important as how long you sleep. Your body has an internal clock that responds to the rising and the setting of the sun. If you have traveled a significant distance in an airplane, you have felt "jet lag." Jet lag is your body's attempt to realign its sleep-and-awake cycle with the new location's daylight and dark periods. Generally, we function best when we sleep at night and stay awake during the day. Check your sleep schedule to see if you are sleeping at a time that will give you the best quality sleep. Try to maintain a consistent schedule. You are interfering with your natural sleep patterns if you constantly change your sleep patterns.

What If You Can't Sleep?

Perhaps you have difficulty falling asleep at night. You lie down in your bed in a darkened room, but you cannot fall asleep. You may begin thinking about the exam you have the next day or the difficulties you are experiencing in a personal relationship. If you are having difficulty falling asleep, try one or more of the following suggestions:

- Sleep in a place that you reserve for sleep. We are creatures of habit. If you save your bed for sleeping rather than reading or watching TV, your body will move into the sleep mode automatically when you lie down.
- Keep your room cool.
- Don't substitute daytime naps for nighttime sleep.

- Take a warm bath or shower before going to bed.
- Reduce your use of caffeine and alcohol. Both impair sound sleep patterns.
- Exercise at least four times per week.
- Use the relaxation techniques suggested in the next section of this chapter.
- Complete your tasks 1 hour before bed so that you can use the hour to unwind and relax.
- Keep a pad of paper and pen next to your bed. Write down any thoughts that are preventing you from relaxing.

CRITICAL REFLECTION EXERCISE

Your Sleep Habits

Sleep is critical to your success. Let's take a minute to compare your sleep habits to those that we have described.

1. If you are getting fewer than 8 hours of sleep per night, are you experiencing any of the sleep deprivation symptoms that we described? If so, what are they?
2. List the times during the day or night when you sleep (be sure to include naps). How much of your sleep is occurring during the daylight hours?
3. List three techniques that you will use when you have difficulty sleeping. ●

Stress

Stress is another component of college life that impacts your ability to think well. A certain amount of stress is beneficial. It keeps you from getting bored. It can focus your attention on a task and stimulate you to respond to that task in a meaningful way. But too much stress can lead to a level of anxiety and worry that not only impacts your ability to think but can also harm you physically. Too much stress can cause loss of sleep, irritability, nausea, loss of appetite, diarrhea, headaches, and ulcers.

Gary Buss/FPG/Getty Images

CRITICAL REFLECTION EXERCISE

Are You Stressed?

The amount of stress you experience is impacted by your current situation in life. The College Readjustment Rating Scale is an adaptation of Holmes and Rahe's Life Events Scale. It has been modified for college-age adults and should be considered a rough indication of stress levels and possible health consequences. In this scale, each event is assigned a value that represents the amount of readjustment a person has to make as a result of the change. In some studies, people with serious illnesses have been found to have high scores on similar scales. To determine your stress score, circle the number of points corresponding to the events you have experienced in the past 6 months or are likely to experience in the next 6 months. ●

The College Readjustment Rating Scale

Event	Points
Death of spouse	100
Female unwed pregnancy	92
Death of a parent	80
Male partner in unwed pregnancy	77
Divorce	73
Death of a close family member	70
Death of a close friend	65
Divorce of one's parents	63
Jail term	61
Major personal injury or illness	60
Flunk out of college	58
Marriage	55
Fired from job	50
Loss of college financial support	48
Failed grade in an important class or required course	47
Sexual difficulties	45
Serious argument with significant other	40
Academic probation	39
Change in major	37
New love interest	36
Increased workload in college	31
Outstanding personal achievement	29
First semester in college	28
Serious conflict with instructor	27
Lower grades than expected	25
Transfer to a new college	24
Change in social activities	22
Change in sleeping habits	21
Change in eating habits	19
Minor violation of law (e.g., traffic ticket)	15

Now add the circled numbers for your score. Persons with scores of 300 and higher have a high health risk. Persons scoring 150–300 points have about a 50-50 chance of serious health change within 2 years. Subjects scoring 150 and below have a one in three chance of serious health change.

Adapted with permission from T. H. Holmes and R. H. Rahe, "The Social Readjustment Scale," in Carol L. Otis and Roger Goldingay, *Campus Health Guide* (New York: CEEB, 1989).

Physical Interventions

If you are experiencing harmful levels of stress, it is time to take action. One way you can address your stress is with physical interventions. When you experience stress, you tend to breathe more quickly and less deeply. If you notice that you are breathing this way, make a conscious effort to change your breathing rate and depth. Slow your breathing rate and deepen the intake of air with each breath.

Your body also responds to high levels of stress by tightening the muscles. You can lower your stress level by using progressive relaxation techniques. Start by tightening the muscles in your feet. Hold that tension for several seconds and then slowly release that muscle tension. Next tighten your calf muscles and hold that tension for several seconds before you release it. Work your way up through the entire body and you will release not only the muscle tension but signal your body to let go of the stress as well.

Exercise is also an important tool you may use to reduce your level of stress. If a low exam score is making you feel tension, do something physical. Go for a bike ride or run. Play basketball or tennis. Physical exercise diminishes your stress.

Psychological Interventions

Stress can also be addressed at the psychological level. Some find that using visualization techniques helps them relax. When a certain circumstance is creating anxiety in your life, find a comfortable place to sit or recline. Draw a picture of that anxiety-producing circumstance in your mind. Then replace it with a more beautiful and peaceful image. That image may be of a beautiful Caribbean beach or a sprawling mountain range. Look at the image you are composing. Immerse yourself in the scents and sounds of that place. Whatever the image, that minivacation of the mind will take you to a place where your body can feel relaxed and refreshed.

Finally, determine what you can and cannot control in your life. There are dimensions of your life that produce stress that you can control. For example, you can control your amount of preparation for an exam. But other things in life are beyond your control. You cannot control whether your boyfriend or girlfriend will stay in a relationship with you. You cannot control the fact that your grandfather has cancer. In those situations, you can cause yourself undue stress and harm by trying to control people or situations that lie outside your power and control.

However, even in circumstances that are out of your control, you can still control the way you respond to them. Your girlfriend or boyfriend may end the relationship, but you can control how you will respond to that rejection. You can talk to others. You can pray about it. You can use relaxation techniques. Those responses make you feel more empowered. And when you feel more in control of your life, your level of stress may be lower.

The suggestions we have offered in this section were designed to reduce your level of stress. You may find that they have not reduced your stress as much as you needed. If that is the case, be sure to seek professional assistance from the counseling office on your campus.

CRITICAL THINKING EXERCISE

Manage Your Stress

Pick a situation in your life that is producing stress and complete the following sentences:

1. What I can control in this situation is . . . .

____

____

2. What I cannot control in this situation is . . . .

____

____

3. What I am going to do to diminish my stress is . . . .

____

____

Diet

"You are what you eat." That old maxim has a lot of truth in it. The body that carries around your brain needs to be nourished. Your brain simply will not function well when it is deprived of nutrients. So we could also say, "You will only think as well as you eat and drink."

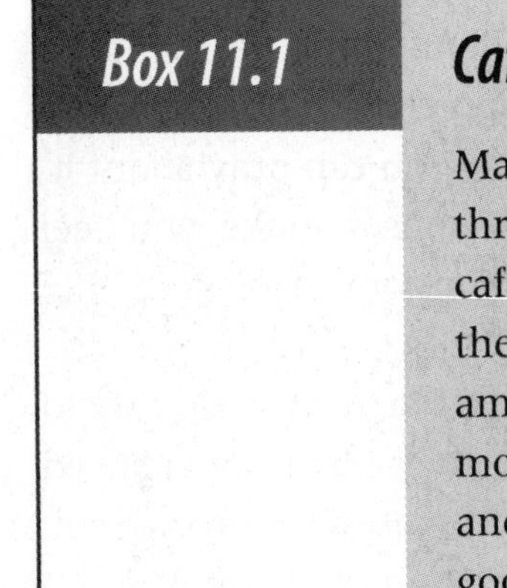

Box 11.1

Caffeine

Many college students seek to manipulate their attentiveness through the use of artificial stimulants such as caffeine. Although caffeine may be the most widely used drug in American society, there is no guarantee that it is working well for you. While a small amount of coffee or a soft drink may help you feel more alert in the morning, it can also produce headaches, nervousness, irritability, and insomnia. One thing is certain. Caffeine is no replacement for a good night's sleep.

How you eat is impacted by your time-management decisions. For example, breakfast is considered by many to be the most important meal of the day. Since your last meal was consumed at least 12 hours earlier, your body is in need of fuel. But some college students have a time-use habit that prevents them from eating breakfast. Their assumption is that 1 more hour of sleep is preferable to getting up for breakfast. This clearly puts them at a thinking disadvantage for the day.

Your body needs to be refueled throughout the day. Hunger is the way your body signals that it needs fuel. You may choose to respond to that hunger with a variety of foods. It is all right to make an occasional stop at the vending machine, but don't be fooled into thinking that just stopping the hunger with junk food means you have given your body what it needs. Your body requires a well-balanced refueling.

CRITICAL REFLECTION EXERCISE

Assess Your Diet

What you eat throughout the day is critical to your success. The U.S. Department of Agriculture has issued guidelines for a healthy diet. We have turned them into a checklist. Put a check next to the standards that are already a part of your healthy eating habit.

- ❑ I eat a variety of foods.
- ❑ My food intake has put me at a healthy weight.
- ❑ My diet is low in fat and cholesterol.
- ❑ I eat plenty of fruits, vegetables, and grain products.

- ❑ I use sugar in moderation.
- ❑ I use salt and sodium in moderation.
- ❑ I use alcoholic beverages in moderation.
- ❑ I need to improve my diet by eating more . . .
- ❑ I need to improve my diet by eating less . . .

Remember, there is a critical link between what you do to your body and how well you are able to think. Restful sleep, effective stress management, and a nutritious diet will put you on the edge of a healthy lifestyle. ●

JOURNAL

Reflect on the circumstances that are producing the most stress in your life. Experiment with the stress management techniques suggested in this chapter. Write about the things causing stress in your life and write about your experience using the stress management techniques. ●

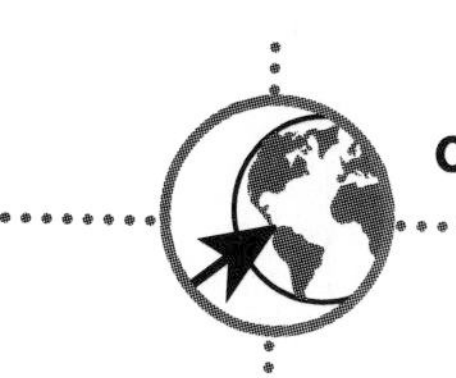

ON THE NET

For more advice and direction on improving the health of your lifestyle, go to Wadsworth's Your College Success Resource Center at www.success.wadsworth.com. Click on "Discipline Resources" and then on "Resource Web Links." Under "Resource Web Links," click on "Assuring Your Physical Health" and "Assuring Your Mental Health." For more dietary guidelines and tips for healthy eating, visit the U.S. Department of Agriculture's Web site at www.usda.gov/cnpp. For more information on stress management, sleep, insomnia, and substance abuse visit www.unc.edu/depts/unc_caps/resources.htm. You can also find additional resources and exercises for *On the Edge of Success* at http://info.wadsworth.com/clason. ●

12

Value Successful Relationships

"Why did she have to break up our relationship the day before my final exam in biology?"

"I am so glad he was here for me. I don't know how I would have made it through the semester without him."

"My parents did it again. They complained about my clothes in front of my friends."

"I don't know what I would have done without my parents. They really got me out of a financial jam last year."

"I hate going to my speech class. The professor intimidates me as soon as she walks into the room."

"I love going to my composition class. My professor really has helped me become a better writer."

College life is full of relationships. And as you can see from these quotes, building and maintaining healthy relationships have a significant impact on your success. That is why relationships are included in the pyramid of success. Near the top of the pyramid, you will find the word "connected." We all need to be connected to other people who support, love, and direct us. Some of your relationships need to be celebrated because they are fostering your climb up the pyramid of success. Other relationships may need to be improved so that they do a better job of fostering your success. Perhaps there is a relationship in your life that needs to be discontinued because it is clearly impairing your ability to succeed.

Which relationships are important to my success?

How can I keep my relationships healthy?

How can I manage conflict in my relationships?

How does diversity enhance my education?

This chapter will help you define the relationships that impact your success and measure the quality of those relationships. It will also discuss how to manage conflict in your relationships and how to build relationships with those who are different from you.

CRITICAL REFLECTION EXERCISE

Define Your Relationships

You have relationships with many different kinds of people. These relationships vary in intensity and importance. Let's draw a picture of the key relationships in your life at the moment. Consider friends, faculty, roommates, family members, casual dates, and significant others. Put yourself in the middle of the circle on page 129. Put the names of the people most important to you in the rings closest to your name and allow less important relationships to drift to the outside rings. After you have placed the names in the rings, take a highlighter in hand. Highlight the relationships that contribute most positively to your success in one color and those that make a more negative contribution in another color. This illustration pictures your relationships and gets you started in the evaluation process. ●

Types of Relationships

Another way to think about your relationships is by considering the types of relationship you are most likely to form. As a partner in a relationship, you seek out either independent, dependent, codependent, or interdependent qualities in another person. Let's define these relationships.

Independent Relationship

The independent partner prefers a very loosely constructed connection. He or she does not want to feel either dependent on or depended on by the other partner. If you give a lot to that person, don't expect to receive the same in return.

Dependent Relationship

The dependent person is just the opposite of the independent personality. The dependent partner wants a very close connection. Since they

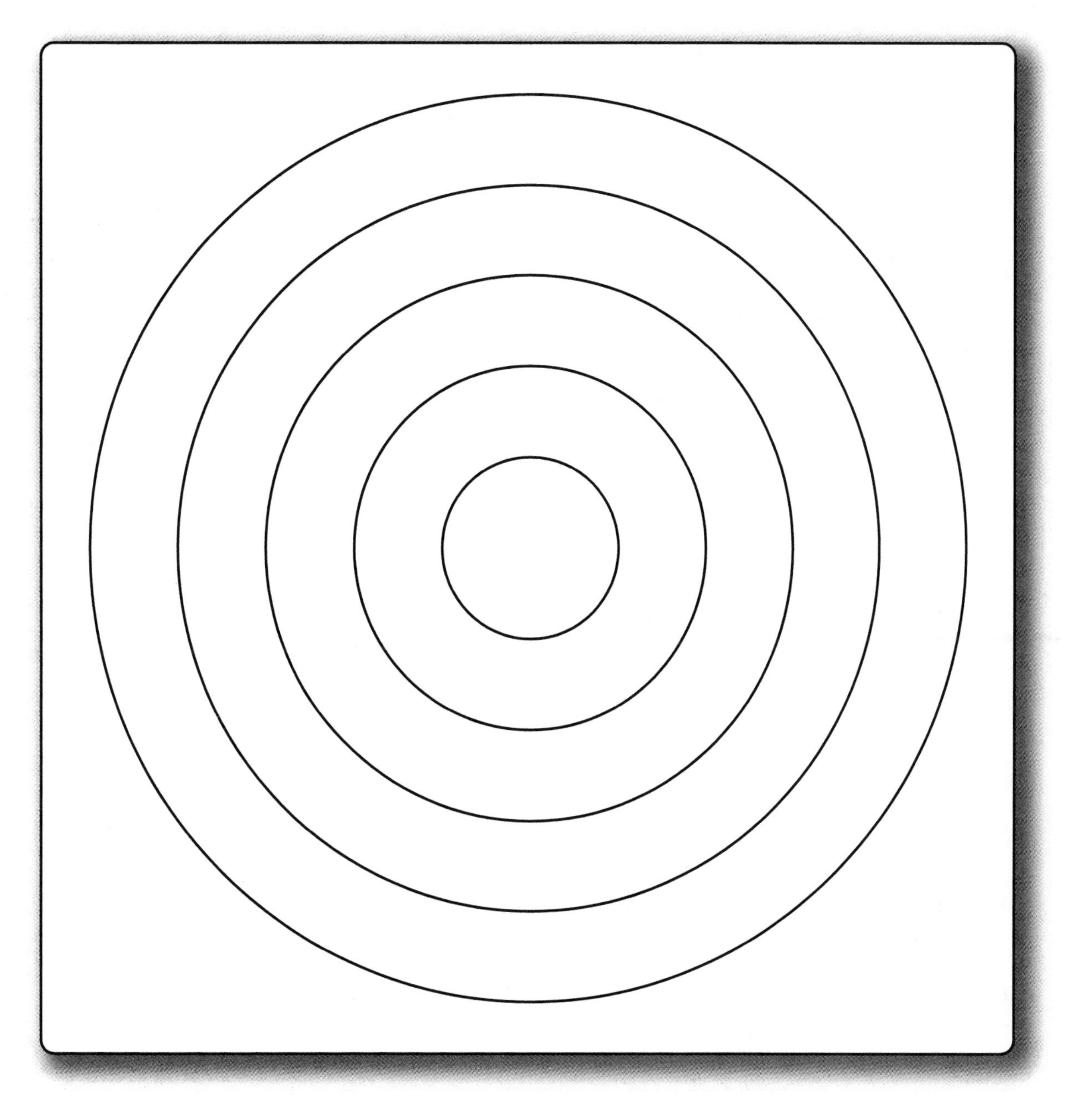

lack the ability to make decisions or function apart from their partner, they may be described as "clinging." This person draws feelings of confidence or self-worth from another.

Codependent Relationship

The codependent person is an extreme caregiver. This person gives more than is healthy for a relationship. This individual wants to make everything okay for everyone. They put significant time and effort into helping others achieve their goals while feeling guilty about taking even a little for themselves.

Interdependent Relationship

The interdependent person strikes a healthy balance between giving and taking. Their sense of self-worth is not linked to others. So they can give without hurting themselves and take without feeling guilty.

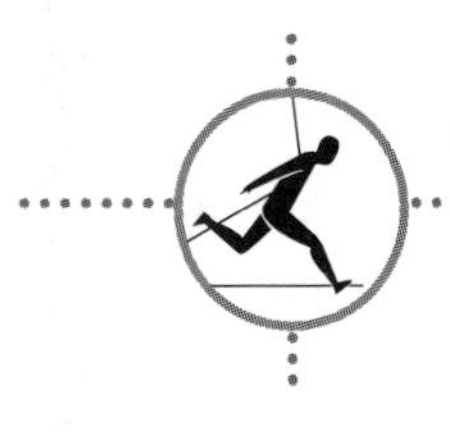

CRITICAL REFLECTION EXERCISE

Who Are You?

Using the information you have just read about the different kinds of relationships, answer the following questions:

What kind of partner do you tend to be? ______________________

What kind of partner do you tend to seek out? ______________________

The Qualities of Healthy Relationships

Even interdependent relationships vary in their level of health. The best personal relationships are built on qualities like the following:

Mutual trust

Mutual respect

Effective communication

Kindness

Patience

Forgiveness

Mutual support

Shared interests

Similar values

CRITICAL REFLECTION EXERCISE

Check Out Your Critical Relationships

To be successful, you need to be connected to a number of persons with whom you share a healthy relationship. Let's put several of your close relationships to the test and see if they are dominated by the

	1	2	3
	___	___	___
I enjoy spending time with him or her.	❑	❑	❑
I trust him or her with personal information.	❑	❑	❑
I can turn to him or her during a difficult time.	❑	❑	❑
He or she respects me and my needs.	❑	❑	❑
I can talk easily and openly with him or her.	❑	❑	❑
He or she is kind to me.	❑	❑	❑
We don't hold grudges.	❑	❑	❑
We bolster each other's self-worth.	❑	❑	❑
We share similar interests and values.	❑	❑	❑

qualities just listed. Put three names on the following lines and a check in the box if your relationship with that person fits the description. ●

Managing Conflict in Relationships

Even the healthiest relationships experience conflict. You and your roommate may have had words over the time the lights get turned out at night. You and your parents may have disagreed over your choice of major. Are you afraid of conflict? You might think that having an argument will hurt the relationship or that it is a signal the relationship itself is bad. You may even fear conflict because you think it might expose some undesirable qualities like meanness, pettiness, or a need to control.

Yet having an argument with a significant other does not automatically hurt the relationship, nor does it mean the relationship is bad. Conflict is an inevitable part of any relationship. It is a product of our being different from one another and not always seeing the world in the same way. The goal is not to avoid conflict but to maintain a healthy relationship even in the midst of conflict.

The first step in managing a conflict involves understanding the very nature of the conflict you are facing. The clash may center on either the content of your conversation or the nature of the relationship itself. For example, let's say that you and your significant other are arguing about the amount of time you spend together. If that conflict centers on the content, it may literally be a disagreement about the number of days and hours you spend together each week. On the other hand, if the conflict is generated by the nature of your relationship, then you may be disagreeing about who is really committed to the relationship. Successful conflict management begins with addressing the true causes of the conflict.

The second step in managing a conflict means looking carefully at the communication habits being employed by the participants. Maybe you never thought that your method of handling a conflict can greatly influence the health of the relationship, but it can. Some habits are helpful. We will call these facilitating communication behaviors. Some habits are harmful to the process of conflict management. We will call these obstructing communication behaviors.

Obstructing Communication Behaviors

Avoiding This is the unwise avoidance of a conflict. It could be either a physical or a mental retreat from the scene or topic, like walking out of the room or ignoring the other person while watching TV. Avoidance is usually harmful; however, if you are being physically or verbally threatened, by all means, retreat from the situation.

Blaming Conflict in a relationship almost always has more than one contributor. When people blame, they make accusations and place all the responsibility for the conflict on their partner.

Uncontrolled Anger It is not wrong to be angry at someone. It is wrong to become so angry that it results in physical or verbal abuse.

Gunnysacking Gunnysackers don't confront the issues as they arise. Instead, they keep long lists of past grievances. When they finally engage their partner on an issue, they may dump all the stored up grievances on their partner. They attack the well-being of their partner even though those past grievances may have nothing to do with the current conflict.

Hitting Below the Belt We are all more sensitive to some issues than others. The person who hits below the belt is not trying to manage the current conflict, but is lashing out in an attempt to hurt his or her partner.

Withholding Sometimes people hope to win an argument by withdrawing their love and affection from their partner.

Inappropriate Joking Humor can be very helpful in diffusing a tense moment. However, inappropriate humor is a form of avoiding that blocks the open exchange of thoughts and feelings. When people joke inappropriately, they may also be sending the message that they do not take the conflict seriously.

Facilitating Communication Behaviors

Engaging in the Conflict Although you may need a "cooling off" period during a conflict, most issues do not get better with age. Confront the issues that are facing you and your partner sooner rather than later.

"I" Messages An "I" message expresses your personal feelings without accusing the other person. For example, saying, "You never let me make my own decisions," will probably provoke the other person to defend him- or herself. Instead, an "I" message would sound like this, "I feel like I need to make my own decision about my major."

Staying Focused Focus on the issues within the present conflict as opposed to bringing up past grievances. Stay focused by seeking clarification from your partner. Are you really listening to what your partner is saying? Is your partner hearing what you are saying? It is critical not to talk past one another.

Apologizing If you have intentionally or unintentionally harmed your partner, say you are sorry. Remember that you only need to apologize for your actions, not your feelings.

Box 12.1

Roommates and Friends

How are your friends and roommates influencing you? Not everyone will be as committed or concerned about your success as you are. If your friends interrupt your study time, encourage you to skip class, or keep you up all night partying, you need to stand up for your best interests. Your friends may not be aware of the impact they are having on you. Speak to them. If they don't listen, make the changes you are empowered to make.

Being Truthful Although the truth may hurt, it deserves to be heard. You may be afraid of hurting someone else by telling the truth. You can still be sensitive to the other person's feelings by stating the truth with kindness.

Finding healthy ways to deal with relationship problems is important. The next time you are involved in a conflict, reflect on whether the conflict centers on content or is about the relationship itself. Then look carefully at the habits you typically use to manage a conflict. Are there obstructing behaviors you need to eliminate? Are there facilitating behaviors you need to foster? For some, it is hard to concentrate on anything else when relational problems arise. If you find that relationship conflict is seriously affecting your ability to succeed, you might want to seek some professional advice.

Diversity

People are important to your success, but not all of the people who contribute to your success look or think like you do. We are different from one another. That difference is at the heart of the college experience. By design, the faculty, staff, and students of a university exhibit both visible and invisible differences. We are a tossed salad of experiences and ideologies. This diverse community challenges you to see the world and its issues through various perspectives. We are challenged to confront new ideas, people, cultural practices, and lifestyles. The exploration of these new ideas is fun and exciting. Campus diversity is a cause for celebration. But let's be certain that your perspective on diversity does not impede your success.

Peter Scholey/FPG/Getty Images

Take a walk through the hallways and down the sidewalks of your school and pay attention to the differences of those you meet. Your walk may bring you into contact with people of a different gender, sexual orientation, religious affiliation, political ideology, age, or race. You may meet someone with a disability, from a different culture, or with a different marital status than you. These are just a few of the differences that exist on campus.

This diversity is designed to enhance your learning experience. But that diversity can produce discomfort, tension, and even fear. Have you been reluctant to seek help from a professor because you felt that the professor would look down on you due to your religious affiliation or race? Has your relationship with your roommate been strained because you felt uncomfortable with his or her sexual orientation or socioeconomic status? Diversity has the potential to create barriers, distrust, and fear. If that has happened to you, try the following:

See your level of comfort with others as a habit and realize that habits can be changed.

Begin changing that habit by stepping out of your comfort zone and intentionally building relationships with people who are different from you. Join a study group with someone of a different religious affiliation. Enjoy an evening out with someone from a different culture.

Before you explore the differences, see the common ground that all humans share. We all need to eat, sleep, love, be loved, and find hope in life. Also seek common ground with personal preferences like music, sports, hobbies, or art. These similarities can increase your comfort with those who are different from you in other ways.

Finally, let your curiosity lead you to appreciate the unique experiences and insights others have to offer.

College life is full of relationships. Everyone needs to feel connected to other people. You have had the opportunity in this chapter to reflect on the relationships in your life and on the quality of those relationships. If you find that your key relationships have weak spots, strengthen them. If you have discovered that there is a severe shortage of people with whom you have healthy relationships, then it is time to pursue new relationships that will provide the support you need. Put the suggestions of this chapter to work in your life and you will be on the edge of successful relationships.

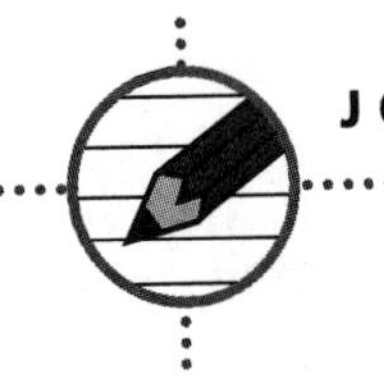

JOURNAL

Write about one or two relationships that are important to your success. In what ways are those relationships strong and where do they need improving? What do you plan to do to keep your critical relationships healthy? ●

ON THE NET

For more advice and direction on building relationships in a diverse world, go to Wadsworth's Your College Success Resource Center at www.success.wadsworth.com. Click on "Discipline Resources" and then on "Resource Web Links." Under the "Resource Web Links," click on "Achieving Relationships in a Multicultural World." For more information on relationship skills, visit www.unc.edu/depts/unc_caps/relationship.htm. You can also find additional resources and exercises for *On the Edge of Success* at http://info.wadsworth.com/clason. ●

13

Step Up to Greater Success

You made a great decision when you decided to come to college. You made a great decision when you decided to stay in college. In the first chapter of this book, we said you were on the edge of success. We asserted that you were not destined to fail. We challenged you to move to greater success by reading the book, doing the exercises, and applying the techniques to your classes. That climb to greater success was no accident. You confronted the challenges that stood in the path of your success. You have worked to change habits and to build on existing strengths. In this chapter, let's review and celebrate your growth.

The pyramid of success makes it clear that success is a product of many components that complement and build on one another. At the base of the pyramid is responsibility. Responsible students are able to own their past mistakes, make a commitment to change, and consistently use the tools and resources available to foster their success. Successful students are also motivated and directed. These students make a personal and emotional investment in their future and direct the energy of their motivation with a plan for success. But successful students also need to feel connected to their community and value themselves for who they are. The capable student is the one who is able to blend these components into a working whole.

How have I changed?

How do I still need to change?

The Pyramid of Success

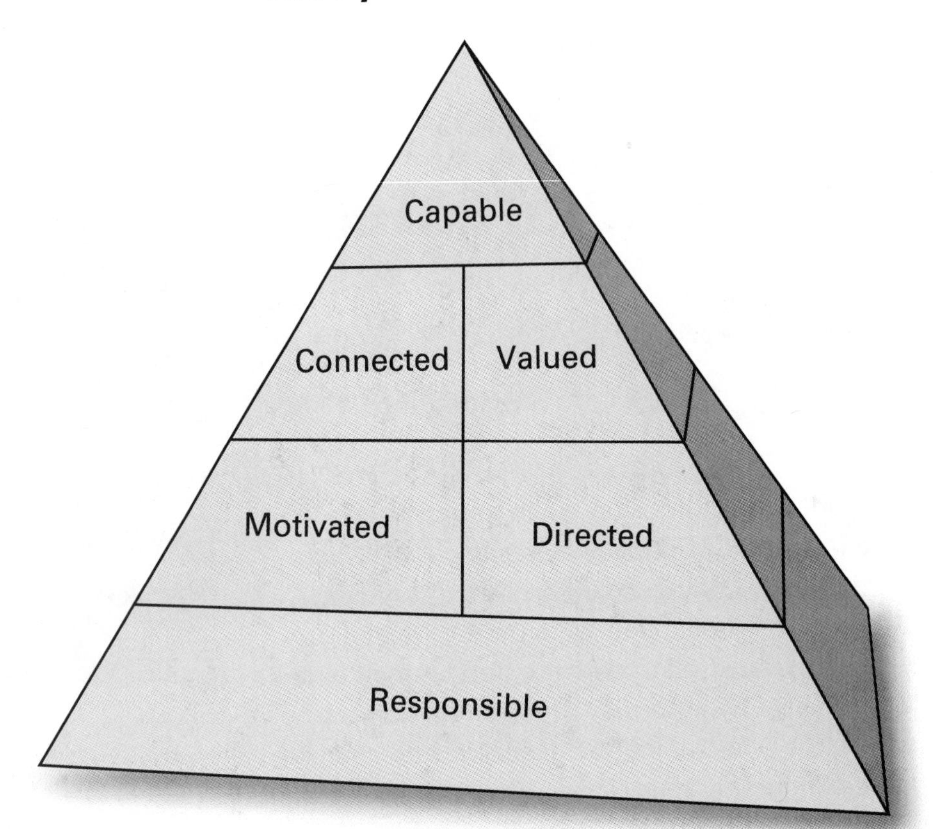

EXERCISE

Your New Pyramid of Success

Earlier in the book, you had the chance to fill in the pyramid of success. Let's see where you are today. Like the exercise in Chapter One, write in the components for success as seen above. Put a highlighter in your hand and visualize yourself climbing the pyramid from bottom to top again. Pause at each level to reflect on your life today. Fill in that percentage of the block you think you have in place. Do that for each step of the pyramid to develop a picture of yourself today. Don't look back at the pyramid in Chapter One until you have completed this pyramid. What changes have taken place? ●

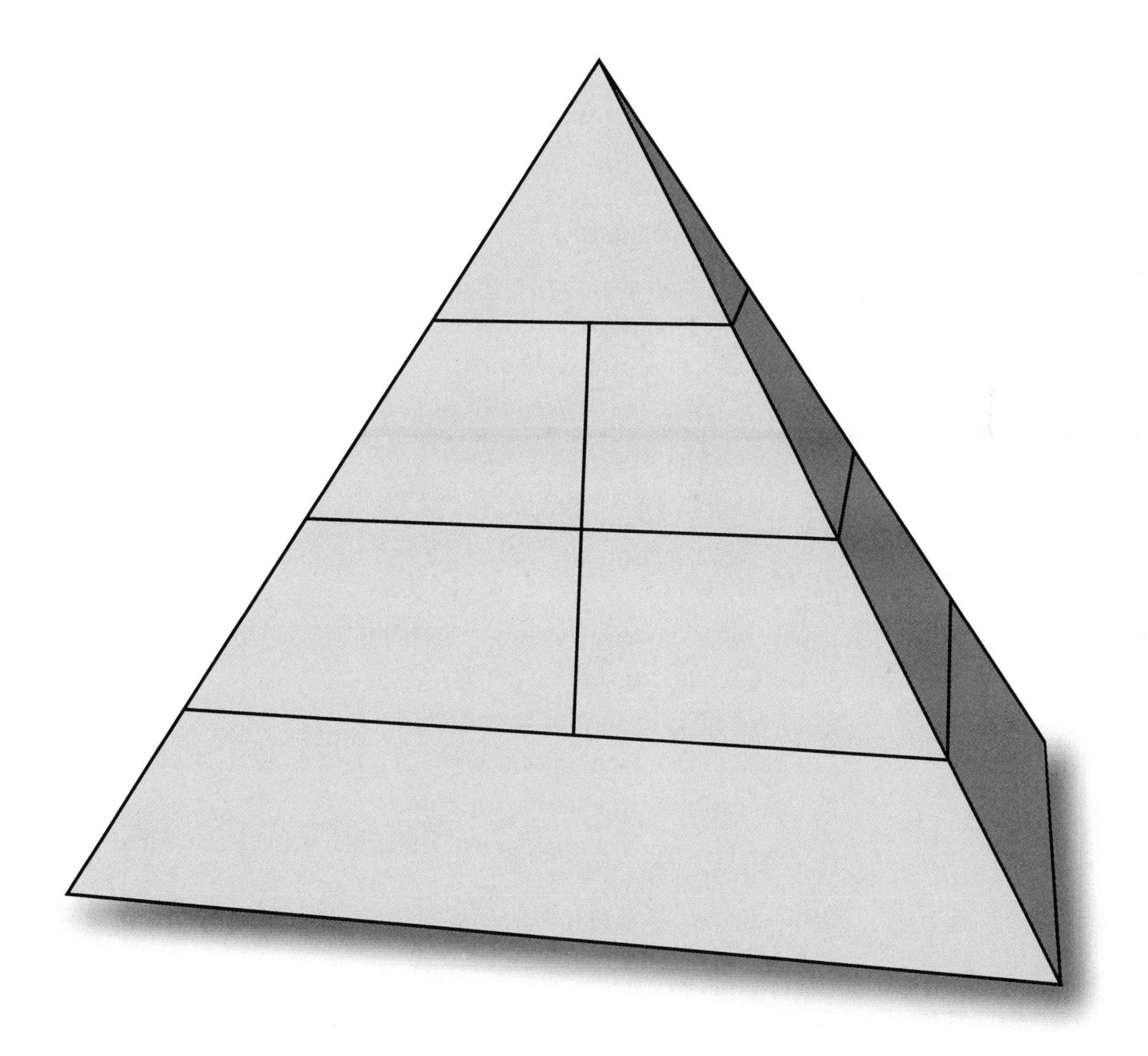

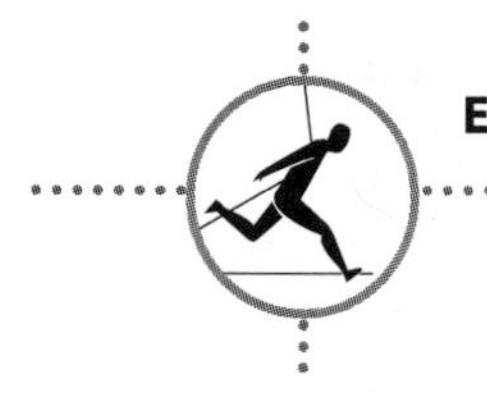

EXERCISE

Your Personal Reassessment

Following is a checklist of habits that may have harmed your chances for success in the past. This is the same list from Chapter Two. It identified challenges in your life that impacted your success. Now that you have made changes in your life, carefully read these statements and review your own habits again. When a statement sounds like you, check it.

Goal Setting and Motivation

- ❑ I am uncertain about my major.
- ❑ I don't feel motivated to do homework.
- ❑ I have trouble setting goals.
- ❑ I have trouble achieving the goals I have set.
- ❑ I don't know what motivates me.
- ❑ I don't have a written plan for success.

Time Management

- ❑ My class attendance needs improvement.
- ❑ I frequently sleep during the day.
- ❑ I have difficulty organizing my work.
- ❑ I have trouble with procrastination.
- ❑ I am easily distracted from my work.
- ❑ I find that sports, parties, or extracurricular activities interfere with my schoolwork.
- ❑ I spend too much time watching TV, playing video games, or surfing the Net.
- ❑ I don't make daily lists of things "to do."
- ❑ I don't make a weekly schedule for work, studying, classes, and free time.

Campus Resources

- ❑ I am nervous about visiting my teachers in their offices.
- ❑ I am unaware of all the support services offered on my campus.
- ❑ I am not sure from which kind of teacher I learn best.

PhotoDisc/gettyimages, 2002

Learning Styles

- ❑ I know that everyone learns differently but I don't know in which ways I learn best.
- ❑ I have a difficult time learning from certain teachers.
- ❑ I don't understand why some people learn more easily than I do.
- ❑ I don't know how to study using my learning strengths.

Reading Strategies

- ❑ I frequently must reread portions of an assignment to understand it.
- ❑ I read too slowly.
- ❑ I don't have a system for remembering what I read.
- ❑ I am easily distracted when I read.
- ❑ I read in the same place that I relax.

- ❑ I don't begin reading the chapter of a book by scanning headings, graphs, and illustrations.
- ❑ I do most of my reading at night.

Note Taking

- ❑ I have trouble paying attention during class.
- ❑ I have only one method of taking notes for all my classes.
- ❑ I don't complete the assigned readings for my classes.
- ❑ Days pass before I review the notes I have taken.
- ❑ I review my notes by reading them over and over again.

Exams

- ❑ I usually start studying for an exam the day before it's given.
- ❑ I don't participate in a study group.
- ❑ I prepare for all my exams by just rereading my notes.
- ❑ I run out of time when taking an exam.
- ❑ My anxiety causes me to forget information that I have studied.
- ❑ I begin all my exams by answering the first question.
- ❑ I stay up very late, sometimes all night, to study for an exam.
- ❑ I have trouble remembering things for an exam.

Writing Papers

- ❑ I am not sure what resources to use when I research a topic in the library.
- ❑ I don't begin writing a paper by writing an outline.
- ❑ I don't reread and edit a paper before I give it to the teacher.
- ❑ My papers receive lower grades because of spelling mistakes or errors in grammar.
- ❑ My papers receive lower grades because they do not flow logically from paragraph to paragraph.
- ❑ I have difficulty picking a topic for some of my papers.
- ❑ I tend to write my papers one or two days before they are due.

Health

- ❑ I have a habit of sleeping during the day and staying up very late at night.

- ❑ I am under a lot of stress and I am not sure what to do with it.
- ❑ I don't have free time planned during my day.
- ❑ I skip breakfast a lot.
- ❑ I don't eat well-balanced meals.
- ❑ I frequently use a stimulant like caffeine to stay awake during the day.
- ❑ Traumatic events from my past are interfering with my ability to succeed today.

Relationships

- ❑ I am homesick.
- ❑ My relationship with my roommates is affecting my grades.
- ❑ I don't have any friends.
- ❑ My friends often get me into trouble.
- ❑ I am afraid to interact with my instructors.
- ❑ My boyfriend/girlfriend depends on me too much.
- ❑ I depend on my boyfriend/girlfriend too much.
- ❑ My family does not support my success.
- ❑ I worry about the health of my relationships. ●

What Else?

Now that you have completed the exercise, compare it to the exercise in Chapter Two to see how you have grown. Write a paragraph on each of these questions:

In what areas have you seen the most improvement?

What areas still need your attention?

What are you going to do to address the areas that still need your attention?

When you first opened this book, you were a different person than you are now. Your circumstances have changed and you have changed. While the review of your life indicates that you are still very much a work in progress, it is clear that you have made some important strides in moving from the edge of success to greater success. You can feel a real sense of pride in what you have accomplished. We celebrate your growth and your step up to greater success.

Keep on climbing!

Photo Credits

Pages 1, 3, 12, 24, 37, 50, 53, 58, 67, 71, 77, 79, 93, 105, 109, 117, 137, 141: PhotoDisc/gettyimages, 2002.

Page 9: Mark Harmel/FPG/Getty Images

Page 17: Rob Brimson/FPG/Getty Images

Page 31: Larry Bray/FPG/Getty Images

Page 45: Rob Goldman/FPG/Getty Images

Page 91: V.C.L./FPG/Getty Images

Page120: Gary Buss/FPG/Getty Images

Page 127: Mark Scott/FPG/Getty Images

Page 135: Peter Scholey/FPG/Getty Images

Index

Notes

Notes

Notes

Notes

Notes

Notes

Notes